Shackleton's Whisky

Shackleton's Whisky

*The extraordinary story of
an heroic explorer and
twenty-five cases of unique
MacKinlay's Old Scotch*

NEVILLE PEAT

preface

Published by Preface 2013

10 9 8 7 6 5 4 3

Copyright © Neville Peat 2013

Neville Peat has asserted his right to be identified as the author of this
work under the Copyright, Designs and Patents Act 1988

First published in Great Britain in 2012 by Preface Publishing

20 Vauxhall Bridge Road
London, SW1V 2SA

An imprint of The Random House Group Limited

www.randomhouse.co.uk
www.prefacepublishing.co.uk

Addresses for companies within The Random House Group Limited can
be found at www.randomhouse.co.uk

The Random House Group Limited Reg. No. 954009

A CIP catalogue record for this book is available from the British Library

ISBN 978 1 84809 390 4

The Random House Group Limited supports The Forest Stewardship
Council® (FSC®), the leading international forest-certification organisation.
Our books carrying the FSC label are printed on FSC®-certified paper.
FSC is the only forest-certification scheme supported by the leading
environmental organisations, including Greenpeace. Our
paper procurement policy can be found at
www.randomhouse.co.uk/environment

Printed and bound in Great Britain by Clays Ltd, St Ives PLC

To those who protect the
Shackleton heritage at Cape Royds

Contents

PART 3 — THE MATCH

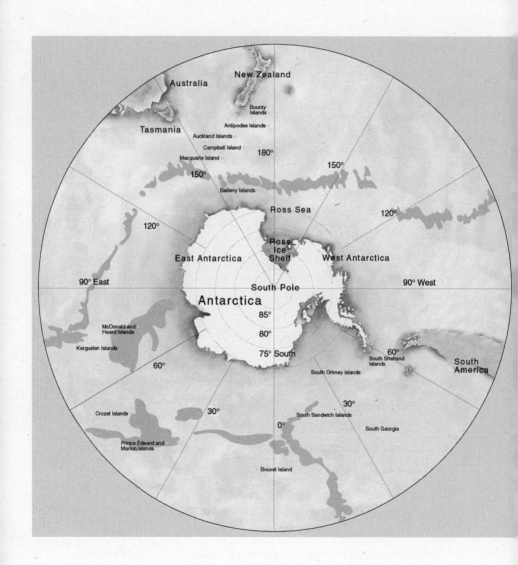

Author's Note

S ir Ernest Shackleton could never have imagined his name being closely associated with whisky, certainly not in the title of a book. Rarely did he consume strong drink. On his expeditions, he tolerated a 'mild spree' at times of celebration. But that was all. Drinking to excess appalled him. From an early age, growing up in a teetotal home, he was leery of alcohol. How, then, did he feel about signing an order for 25 cases of whisky — 300 bottles — for his 1907–09 British Antarctic Expedition?

This book follows the circular story of the Rare Old Highland Malt Whisky taken south on his Nimrod expedition. It celebrates the extraordinary achievements of men exploring an extraordinary place. It dips into the human-interest stories of polar life in the 'heroic era' of Antarctic exploration. At times, the view is up-close and personal. Shackleton once wrote of his interest in documenting 'the little incidents that go to make up the sum of the day's work, the humour and the weariness, the inside view of men on an expedition'. Here is one such account, based largely on what he wrote and said about the expedition and also on what the members of his expedition wrote, for most participants kept a diary or journal.

Shackleton's world fame is founded on the Endurance expedition of 1914–17, an attempt to cross the Antarctic continent that was foiled by the crushing of the ship in pack ice. The heroics that followed ensured Shackleton and his men would have a place forever in the annals of polar history and world exploration at large, even though they were a long way from setting foot on the continent. His Nimrod expedition, seven years earlier, targeted the South Pole from the opposite side of Antarctica, generating a public aura akin to a 1960s lunar landing. At Cape Royds in the McMurdo Sound region stands the only tangible evidence of Shackleton in Antarctica: his hut, under which, until recently, lay a long-kept secret.

Antarctic exploration and whisky, in their own way, are both steeped in history, maturity, endurance, character, and edgy technology. Both have a worldwide following, millions of fans. Their pathways coincided on the British Antarctic Expedition 1907–09. With the recovery 100 years later of three cases of Scotch from icy entombment under the hut at Cape Royds and the subsequent return of three bottles to Scotland for sampling, analysis and a near-magical replication, the relationship of whisky and Antarctic exploration came sharply into focus. All of which makes for a unique odyssey to the end of the Earth and back.

Neville Peat, *Broad Bay, Dunedin, New Zealand, August 2012*

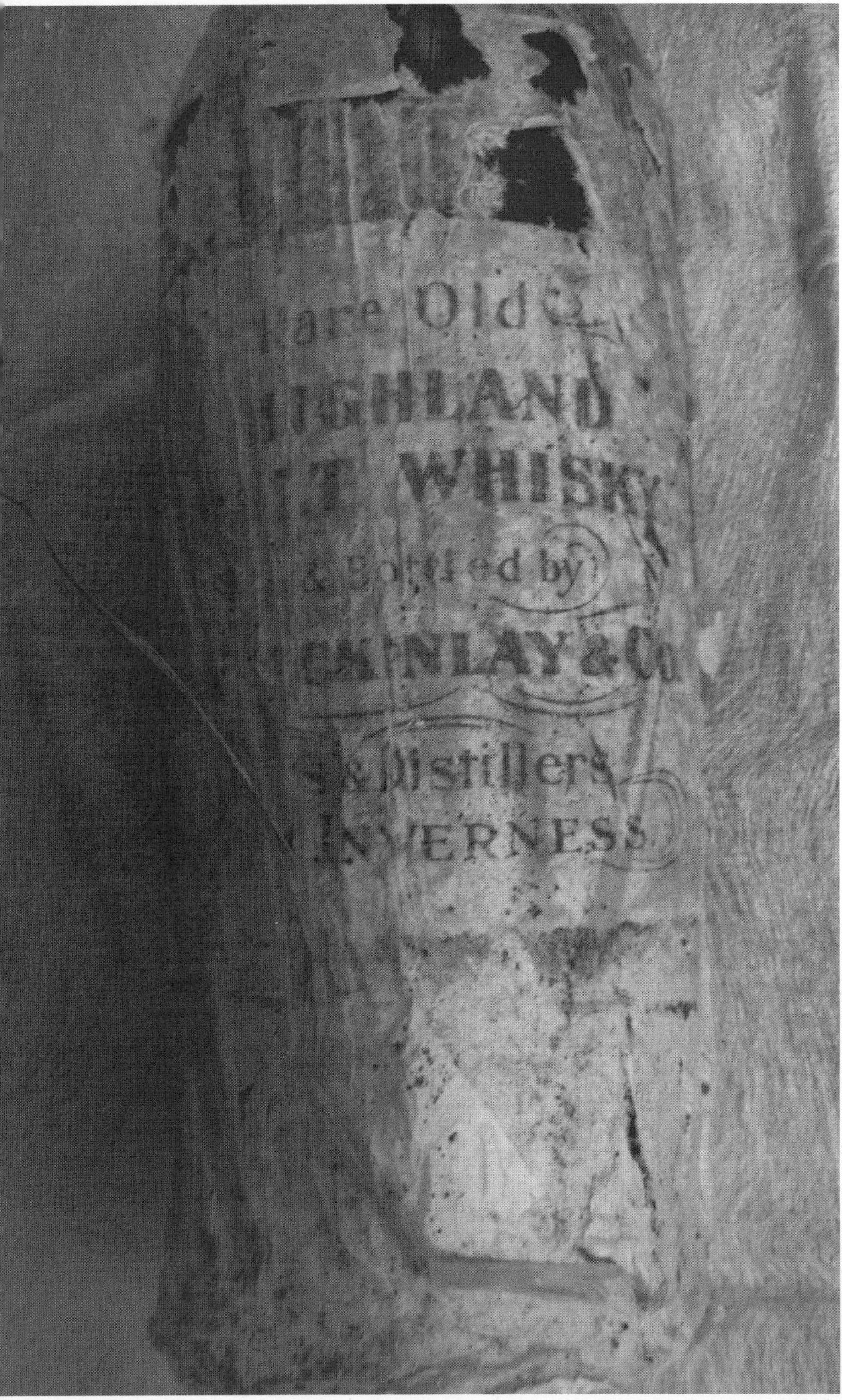
Old
IGHLAND
T WHISK
ed by
INLAY & Co
Distillers
INVERNESS

Prologue

On a sunlit gem of a day that is cold enough to form rime ice on a beard, 'diamond dust' is something to marvel at. It occurs when sunshine bounces off crystals of water vapour suspended in the air. A sparkling fairyland effect is the result. In Antarctica, watch out, too, for other tricks of light and atmosphere. Mock suns in summer, lunar haloes in winter and mirages for much of the year. Two peaks where only one is mapped. Islands elevated. Penguins that appear suspended in mid-air.

Yet water vapour is not an obvious feature when you visit Ross Island, McMurdo Sound. Here it never rains and rarely snows. Blizzards are filled with dry powder snow blown from elsewhere, and in the sunless depths of winter the air may be cold enough to crack metal.

The day I fly to Cape Royds, Ross Island — an address straight out of the heroic era of Antarctic exploration — summer is full blown. Virtually cloudless, blindingly bright, uncommonly still. It is early January 2007.

With temperatures near zero, or even a bit above that, the day is too warm for diamond dust. Nonetheless, a fine day in the McMurdo Sound region is a glittering sensation. Look around.

Mount Erebus is the great hulking centrepiece of Ross Island, its summit often generating a plume of pale blue smoke and steam. But not this day. Is there a lid on it? In the astonishingly clear air, any thought that this could be an active volcano reaching a breathtaking 3794 metres — higher than Aoraki Mount Cook in New Zealand and topped by a lake of boiling lava — seems preposterous. Scale is deceptive. Forty kilometres away? Surely not. From Scott Base at the foot of elongate Hut Point Peninsula, which forms Ross Island's southern tip, Erebus looks like a large local hill, an easy climb.

To the south and east lies the enormous white flatness of the Ross Ice Shelf, the 'Barrier' to the South Pole for the heroic-era explorers from Britain who came here. Picture a creeping wall of ice 80 to 100 metres thick and as large as France shouldering a volcanic doorstop, Ross Island. Something has to give. The leading edge of the great wall is crumpled into radiating waves and steep pressure ridges, metres high.

To the southwest, the Royal Society Range stands stately, Mount Lister the tallest of its peaks, topping 4000 metres. On the western flank of McMurdo Sound, lying behind a skirt of piedmont ice, are the Dry Valleys. Three sprawling valley systems here comprise the greatest expanse of bare rock in all of Antarctica.

At McMurdo Sound, therefore, nature's forces have put together an unbelievably diverse and dynamic array of landforms and ice features, concentrated on the world's southernmost port for shipping, the leaping-off place to the South Pole by air or overland.

My week's assignment in January 2007 coincides with the breakout of sea ice in McMurdo Sound. Sea ice comes and goes in an annual cycle, forming through winter and spring to a thickness of about two metres. No two years are quite the same, and generally ice-breakers have round-the-clock work to do at Christmas and New Year, cutting a channel for cargo and fuel ships directly to the ice wharf at McMurdo Station, the American base.

As it was for explorers Scott and Shackleton in the early years of the 20th century, the sea ice is a critical factor for modern expeditions, which depend on a pattern of summer sunshine and periodic gales to weaken and disperse it. The ships of the two eras might be worlds apart in design, manufacture and kit. But here, natural forces will be nothing less than formidable.

When I take to the air from Scott Base with New Zealand helicopter pilot Rob McPhail, McMurdo's sea ice beyond Hut Point Peninsula is revealed as a seamless extension of the ice shelf. White, relentlessly white, bordering on painfully so.

The blunt-nosed Iroquois continues climbing. I have an altitude in mind — whatever it takes for a view of both Antarctic bases, Scott and McMurdo. In my experience of this region, going back 30 years, I have never seen an oblique photograph of the two stations in their volcanic landscape. Separated by a hilly three kilometres, the stations, built near sea level, are obscured from each other. My commission is to produce a book celebrating 50 years' cooperation between New Zealand and the United States in Antarctica, and the least I can do is try to illustrate the proximity of the stations.

At 700 metres above the ice, frozen snow and black rock, the Scott Base complex of linked green buildings turns into a child's plaything. McMurdo is in the distance now, the only town in Antarctica, nothing decorative, unashamedly functional. These days there are multicoloured recycling bins strategically placed around town.

I have my aerial picture. Pity to intrude on such a serene day with a helicopter's clatter.

There is more to come. A film crew is heading for Captain Scott's hut at Cape Evans, a short flight up the coast. I can hitch a ride with them to Cape Evans, and fly on to Cape Royds on a routine mail and supplies run.

The channel through the sea ice, arrow straight, is closer now. The United States Coast Guard ice-breaker *Polar Sea* is busy tidying the edges, its Santa Claus-red hull no doubt a cheering sight around Christmas for the ice-bound scientists and station personnel. Conditions here, in winter if not in summer, are about as close to being on another planet as anywhere on Earth — extremely cold and dry.

Approaching Cape Evans, we pass the extraordinary Erebus Ice Tongue, a floating extension of the Erebus Glacier. Maps of Ross Island present it as a gigantic sword, both edges jagged. Now comes a cluster of islands, Tent, Inaccessible, Big Razorback, Little Razorback — names applied by the earliest explorers around a century ago.

Shackleton's Antarctic lair looms. Eleven kilometres north of Cape Evans and about halfway up Ross Island's east coast, Cape Royds is the island's eastern promontory, the closest land to the continent proper. We are over open water now, with angular scraps of sea ice randomly scattered. These floes act as lifeboats for penguins trying to escape predators like orca and leopard seals.

The water is the deepest blue imaginable. It seems an appropriate intensity of colour for sea surrounding such a darkly mysterious and unfathomable continent.

Penguins in sight! Yes, the Cape Royds Adelie penguin colony: dark dots among guano patches that are tinged sienna and krill-pink. Thirty years ago, out of respect for the world's southernmost penguin colony, a helicopter might not have flown over the Adelie penguins at their breeding clusters fringing the headland; but the rowdy machines did land within 'cooee' of the birds, on rising ground nearby. Not so now. Antarctic Treaty strictures are in effect. We approach by air today through Backdoor Bay and land out of sight of the penguins.

From the helipad it is a five-minute walk to the seat of Ernest Shackleton's expedition — a pilgrimage many desire to make but few manage.

Free at last of the engine noise, I walk past a silent huddle of orange polar tents and a large blue kitchen-dining tent, accommodation for a New Zealand Antarctic Heritage Trust conservation team. There is no one at home. It is the middle of a working day down at the hut. I crest a low ridge, and suddenly before me is a showcase of Antarctic heritage, both natural and built.

Standing out in a rocky hollow overlooking ice-encrusted Pony Lake, with nesting penguins fanned out on the far side of the lake and the white-fringed cobalt sea beyond, is the hallowed hut, home and castle of the British Antarctic Expedition 1907–09. Ernest Shackleton and 14 hand-picked men were based here for 13 months.

More cottage than castle, it was the wellspring of daring feats of exploration and scientific achievement in the coldest place on Earth. As I look down on the little dwelling in its picturesque setting, I try to make sense of it a hundred years on.

Compared with the sprawl of McMurdo Station and even compact Scott Base, the footprint of this hut is astonishingly small, no larger than that of a 50-seat tourist coach. Yet here was an expedition of numerous 'firsts' — first ascent of Mount Erebus, first attainment of the Magnetic South Pole and a new Farthest South that almost gained the Geographic South Pole, numerous firsts in earth and life sciences, first ponies and first motor vehicle in Antarctica, and first book-publishing venture on the frozen continent, titled *Aurora Australis*.

On this fine midsummer's day, men are working at makeshift benches in an outdoor carpentry shop, roofless because no rain is either forecast or possible. They are engaged in the preservation and restoration of a priceless Antarctic heirloom, the Nimrod Hut, named after Shackleton's ship.

The staggering human interest of this site overpowers the surrounding and not inconsiderable biophysical features — the Adelie colony draped over a line of low sea cliffs, the lake with its summer moat edges, the bare black scoria underfoot and the fantastic volcanic outcrops weathered to wacky forms.

Look behind: Mount Erebus is a lot closer now, more powerful and brooding, its summit hard-etched into the azure sky and still plume-less.

I have an hour here, time only for snap impressions. At the outdoor workshop someone is bent over a wooden door made of freshly tooled and appropriately aged and weathered Scots pine timber. A replica of the original door, it will replace a modern

A new replica door being installed at the Nimrod Hut, January 2007. James Blake (left) is assisting carpenter Steve Brown.
NEVILLE PEAT

equivalent. Before I leave, the replica will be installed. History refurbished, just like that. This outer door of Shackleton's hut is highly symbolic. It marks an exceptional threshold — outside it, an environment too extreme for humans; within it, a haven where men once socialised and steeled themselves for exploration in the frozen unknown.

Atop a nearby knoll is the original wooden structure for the expedition's weather station, and beside the sheltered and sunlit north wall of the hut are the preserved remains of dog kennels, packing cases, and hay bales for the expedition ponies. At the foot of the sunny north wall, on hands and knees and scrabbling in what looks like a pile of rubbish — in reality, historic treasure — I find 20-year-old James Blake. He is holding a small tin box, grimy and newly excavated. Inside it are matches, appearing well preserved. Some pieces of harness have also been removed from the frozen scoria. James is on a month's assignment to assist the conservation team. He represents the Auckland-based Sir Peter Blake Trust, founded in memory of his father to foster youth leadership and encourage environmental good deeds.

The chatter of penguin parents attending to half-grown chicks wafts in with the guano scent, but I am attracted indoors now, through a porch, past Mawson's lab on one side and Wild's storeroom on the other, and so into the main room of the Nimrod Hut. Shackleton's 'cabin' is around to the right. The room is museum-tidy, a sanctuary. There are multiple bunk areas and abandoned workaday items everywhere, too many to take in.

At the far end is the Smith & Wellstood coal stove, a warm brown colour now, the expedition hearth. It burnt coal and seal blubber continuously. Without it they would not have survived. All around the interior, on shelving, are leftover supplies of tinned food and other essentials. For a hut abandoned for nigh on a century, it is well stocked.

My hour is almost up. Time to fly out. New Zealand caretakers and conservation teams have worked here since 1960, and in recent years the Christchurch-based Antarctic Heritage Trust has lifted the conservation effort. The Nimrod Hut, lovingly restored and secured for decades to come, is a tribute to their commitment, not to mention to that of Shackleton and his men.

Since November 2006, a web camera mounted nearby has sent real-time satellite pictures of the hut and its setting to Internet watchers at large. Given this age of instant information, it is surprising no photographs or announcements quickly emerged of a discovery of world interest in the 2006–07 summer, actually in the same week as my visit. An Antarctic Heritage Trust team member, digging deep, confirmed that a couple of wooden whisky cases entombed in ice underneath the floor of the Nimrod Hut were not empty; they really did contain bottles. The footprint had guarded an intoxicating secret for 100 years!

Modern Antarcticans party a lot, especially around midwinter, Christmas and birthdays. Did Shackleton's men celebrate these festive occasions — not to mention their feats of exploration, survival and scientific discovery — in Bacchanalian style? Whisky, brandy, champagne and other forms of strong drink came ashore with them. Ernest Shackleton had ordered 25 cases of Rare Old Highland Malt Whisky for the Nimrod expedition — 300 bottles in all. That equates to 20 bottles for each of the 15 members of the shore party, minus whatever was drunk on the voyage to Cape Royds. Plenty has been written about the course of the expedition and its spectacular achievements; its social life has had less attention. Shackleton concluded that an Antarctic explorer of his

MACKINLAY'S
Rare Old
HIGHLAND MALT WHISKY

The Enduring Spirit

MACKINLAY'S RARE OLD HIGHLAND MALT WHISKY
WAS THE SPIRIT THAT FORTIFIED SHACKLETON'S
'NIMROD' EXPEDITION TO ANTARCTICA IN 1907.
THIS COMMEMORATIVE RE-CREATION CELEBRATES
THE ENDURING HEART AND CHARACTER OF BOTH
MAN AND WHISKY. IT IS THE SPIRIT OF ANOTHER TIME.

ML
Rare Old
HIGHLAND
MALT WHISKY
Blended & Bottled by
CHAS. MACKINLAY & Co
Blenders & Distillers
LEITH & INVERNESS

era, wintering over, could 'learn more about human nature than he ever learnt from this ice fastness'.

For any casual visitor to the Nimrod Hut, intriguing questions abound. How were the materials for the hut and hundreds of cases landed? There is no handy beach. How did the men cope with living in such a confined space? What did they eat? How did they while away their time through the winter darkness? Socially, was it all smooth sailing? 'A very happy little party' was how Shackleton portrayed the experience. But what was it like, really?

In 1908, the interior of the Nimrod Hut was an isolated, pulsating capsule of human interest in a desert of permafrost, snow and ice. A hundred years on, thanks to intensive conservation efforts, the hut is frozen in time. There are no tricks of the light inside it. What you see is more or less what they got, how they lived, how they endured this faraway and at times fearsome place.

'Men go out into the void spaces of the world for various reasons. Some are actuated simply by the love of adventure, some have the keen thirst for scientific knowledge, and others are drawn by "the lure of little voices", the mysterious fascination of the unknown. I think in my own case it was a combination of these factors that determined me to try my fortune once again in the frozen south.'

Ernest Shackleton, *The Heart of the Antarctic*, 1909

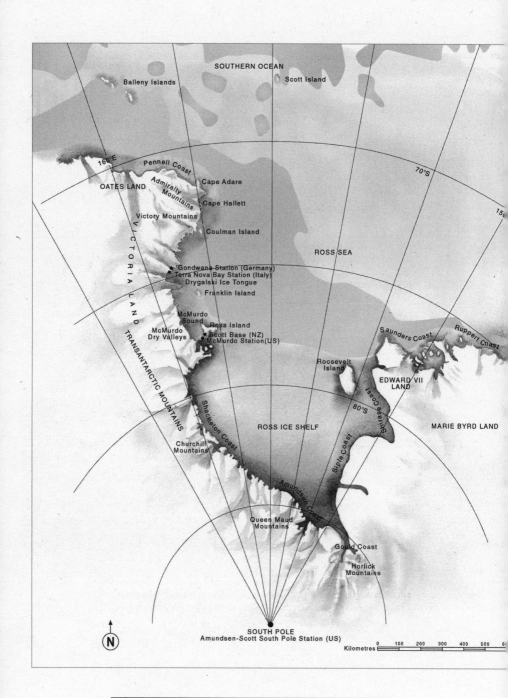

The Ross Sea Region, from Cape Adare to the South Pole,
featuring the Ross Ice Shelf (the Great Ice Barrier), Ross Island,
McMurdo Sound and the Trans-Antarctic Mountains.
ANTARCTICA NEW ZEALAND

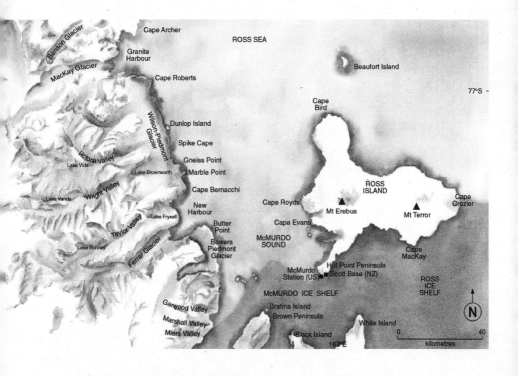

The McMurdo Sound Region, featuring Cape Royds, Mt Erebus, Cape Crozier and Hut Point Peninsula, with the Dry Valleys on the western side of the sound.
ANTARCTICA NEW ZEALAND

PART
1
THE
Order

1 —
INITIATIVES

Towards the end of the 19th century, the twilight years of the Victorian era, steam was overhauling sail at sea, and on land electricity and motor vehicles were bringing revolutionary change to city life and industry in Britain. In 1897, Queen Victoria and her subjects — 'my beloved people' — celebrated her 60th year as monarch. Her empire was vast, covering a fifth of the Earth's land area, and her navy supreme. British merchant shipping was also pervasive, trading to the world's most exotic and distant ports.

Rising through the merchant ranks, a second officer on Shire Line tramp steamers plying to the Far East and across the Pacific to the Americas, Ernest Shackleton, by 1897, had already served seven years in merchant ships, fresh-faced and straight out of Dulwich College, a London public (i.e. private) school for boys. The Merchant Navy was a reality check for a Christian lad thrust suddenly into a world where hard liquor, foul language and drunken behaviour were habitual on voyages that took months to complete.

In the middle of Queen Victoria's Diamond Jubilee year Shackleton took shore leave in London, and glimpsed unrelated opportunities for romance and polar exploration. The first unfolded at the family home in Sydenham, South London, when one of his sisters, introduced him to a friend of hers, Emily Dorman. The daughter of a well-off London solicitor, Emily was tall and beautiful and, at 28, five years older than Edith's brother. Shackleton was immediately attracted to her and, in keeping with his charming and assertive nature, he made his interest known. But the sea's pull won out. Before long he was away again on a tramp steamer, although not before newspaper reports previewed a different kind of voyage originating in Antwerp, the Belgian port across the Dover Strait.

A converted whaling ship, the *Belgica*, was about to leave for the Antarctic Peninsula via Punta Arenas in southern Chile on a voyage of scientific discovery, the first of its kind. Two years earlier the first landing on the Antarctic continent proper had occurred on the other side of Antarctica, in the sector south of New Zealand. Footprints were made on the gravel beaches at Cape Adare, northern Victoria Land. But this new Belgian quest was intriguing. *Belgica* planned to winter over in sea ice to advance Antarctic research, an untapped field. Her officers included an adventurous young Norwegian named Roald Amundsen. At the thought of this polar initiative, something stirred in the Shire Line second mate: the promise of opportunity and discovery at the end of the Earth.

Shackleton's shore leave did not coincide with the royal jubilee celebrations and public outpourings for the ageing monarch, who had returned to London by horse-drawn carriage and steam train from Balmoral Castle in Scotland. He missed the epoch-making occasion — a record reign — by a week. Around the same time, deeper into the Highlands region than Balmoral and without any fanfare whatsoever, a state-of-the-art whisky distillery was going about a business centuries old. In the summer of 1897, at the Glen Mhor distillery in seaside Inverness, distillations of malt whisky were taking shape. Ten years on, Shackleton would make contact with it — Highland whisky.

2 —
TEMPERANCE, TENNYSON AND SEA TIME

The Shackleton family has roots in Ireland; they are not as old as whisky's origins in Scotland, but they do go back a long way. About 1720, Abraham Shackleton arrived in Ireland from the western edge of Yorkshire with his wife and children. He had been invited there by a Quaker community at Ballitore, County Kildare, southwest of Dublin. The area was known for its Anglo-Irish history. A Quaker himself and a teacher, Abraham founded a school in the area. Five generations on, Ernest Henry Shackleton was born at Kilkea, a few miles south of Ballitore, on 15 February 1874, the second child and elder son of Henry Shackleton and his wife, Henrietta. His mother, a warm-hearted woman, had Irish ancestry tracing back to the 12th century. Ernest's heritage was indelibly Yorkshire Quaker and Irish, a family of teachers, landowners, educated and religious folk.

His grandfather, also named Abraham, became interested in the family's English history, and from a cousin living in London he acquired a copy of the Shackleton coat of arms, portraying a shield

Ernest Shackleton.
BERESFORD, LONDON;
THE HEART OF THE ANTARCTIC

and ruffled cape topped by a poplar tree. An amended version was approved by heraldry authorities in Dublin for the Irish branch of the family, with the motto *Fortitudine vincimus* — By endurance we conquer.

When Ernest was born, his father was farming leased land at Kilkea. Then came a slump. Prices for farm products, especially grain, were hit by a recession in the mid-1870s, and in 1880 Henry Shackleton moved his family to Dublin. He began studying medicine. It was a career shift that prompted a further move to London in 1884, where he set up in practice as a doctor. England was not unfamiliar to him because he had been sent by his parents to school in Wellington, Somerset. By the time Henry Shackleton moved to London he had left the Quaker movement and joined the Church of England, and was bringing up his 10 children in tune with Anglican values and doctrine.

Ernest was now 10, an inquisitive lad of strong build, with slate-blue eyes, thick dark hair and a moderate Irish accent. Despite the disruption of moving to Dublin and London he grew up in a secure family setting, with a nurse through his toddler years and a teacher-governess later, till the age of 11. Over the next two years he attended Fir Lodge Preparatory School, then enrolled at Dulwich College as a day-boarder in 1887 — Queen Victoria's Golden Jubilee year. The college was within walking distance of the family's home, Aberdeen House, in middle-class Sydenham.

Ernest and his siblings — a brother and eight sisters — relished the confidence and mutual support of a caring family with a strong, instructive father figure. Henry Shackleton also communicated a love of poetry, and Ernest was all ears for Tennyson, Shelley and Keats. Their poetry fuelled an active imagination. By the time Ernest was born, Alfred, Lord Tennyson had already inspired a generation. He was Poet Laureate for four decades of the Victorian era, the Queen's favourite poet.[1]

From his schoolboy years Ernest doted on the poems about life, love and heroism that sprang from the great English poets of the 19th century. He was a treasure hunter, seeking out literary finds and eager to tell his siblings about his discoveries. He was also a campaigner, treading moral pathways. Even though his father had turned away from Quaker society, that did not mean Quaker values were of no account. A sharing and egalitarian society, pacifism and non-violence, tolerance of cultural diversity, temperance: these, among other ideals, touched the young Shackleton, and he decided they were worth promulgating. Temperance was close to being top of his list. In his boyhood, English and Irish society tended to embrace liquor as a sustaining fact of life, up there with water and food. Liquor had medicinal value. It could produce a healthy glow. But to a thinking Christian or Quaker liquor was identified as a scourge in society that aided and abetted violence, domestic disorder, social disunity and poverty.

In the Shackleton home at Sydenham, which was teetotal as far as family members were concerned, the elder son tried out his message against strong drink. He lectured the servants about it. According to his first biographer, Hugh Robert Mill, young Ernest persuaded the home help to sign up to a pledge of abstinence. He did this, says Mill, by 'his irresistible willingness of appeal'. He had charisma.

Ernest also took his temperance campaign to the streets, where he applied direct action. He joined street parades that demonstrated with banners against the evils of alcohol, and he led his older sisters on gatherings outside pubs, where they would remonstrate and raise their voices in anti-liquor chants and songs.

Temperance societies were on the march. The Band of Hope, a Christian movement, achieved a high profile. Formed in 1847, it built up a huge membership during the second half of the 19th century. Ernest Shackleton, if not a flag carrier for the Band of Hope, was an ardent supporter.

This role as an advocate and activist for sobriety did not stand in the way of his natural instincts for humour and teasing. The elder brother had plenty of fun in him, and his sisters were often on the receiving end of his jokes.

Dulwich College, founded in 1618, was, for most of his four years of secondary schooling, no joke, though. He entered the boys' college at 13, no doubt with his father's expectations riding on him for a working life in medicine. But college studies and Ernest Shackleton did not gel. He became bored by much of the academic work, although he revelled in sports and physical education. Books about overseas adventure and distant cultures caught his attention, and poetry provided light relief from the dry old classroom fare. Biographer Mill, who became his friend and mentor after his first trip to Antarctica, described his class rankings till the last year as 'south of the equator and sometimes perilously near the Pole'.

In the last term of his final year at Dulwich, 1890, his academic performance reached more equable latitudes. In history and literature he came second in his class, and in chemistry third. In mathematics he finished in third place in a class of 25. This was encouraging for a 16-year-old who was thinking of going to sea, given the importance of mathematics in navigation.[2]

Henry Shackleton's dream of a son and heir following him into medicine gave way to the son's sea fever. Ernest did not run away to sea, as a memoir writer once suggested. No: a Shackleton relative arranged an apprentice position on a White Star Line clipper, *Hoghton Tower*, for a shilling a month. He joined the ship at Liverpool bound for romantically distant Valparaiso, Chile, with his Bible packed away safely so he could continue with his readings from it. He took poetry books as well into the hard-bitten life of a merchant seaman. On that first voyage, Shackleton would later declare, he learnt more about geography than if he had stayed at school until the age of 80.

> *To sail beyond the sunset, and the baths*
> *Of all the western stars, until I die.*
> — from 'Ulysses' by Alfred, Lord Tennyson

He never looked back, despite the storms — he saw a crewman washed overboard and was almost lost overboard himself in huge seas in the Pacific Ocean — the rough work of scrubbing decks and polishing brass, seedy ports, arduous cargo handling, wet clothes, lumbago, dysentery, homesickness and the rough and boozy company. His shipmates eventually came to accept him as a poetry-loving bookworm. Some even admired him. In a letter home, though, he told about acquiring a smoking habit: cigarettes. There was no mention of falling for the vice of liquor. Nor would his family expect any such mention.

In 1894, turning 20, the apprentice began his rise through officer ranks. He became third officer on a White Star steamer returning from America. From that voyage he turned up at the family home in Sydenham with a collection of baby alligators, claiming them to be pets. The prankster elder son had returned home. The maids at Aberdeen House 'freaked'.

Third Officer Shackleton was developing a more robust

physique, and to go with it an edge for giving orders. Any Irish brogue left in him had been diminished by his years at Dulwich College and further moulded by international travel. He now had a cultivated English accent that reflected an assertive nature. As for his personality, he never lost his softer, compassionate side. As a friend said, he was 'a Viking with a mother's heart'.

In 1896, he passed his Master's certificate at Singapore. This led to his promotion to second officer and more voyages. His introduction the following year to Emily Dorman blossomed with successive bouts of shore leave. Emily followed the arts, theatre, singing and poetry. Robert Browning entranced her, and her handsome, square-jawed sailor-suitor soon became a devotee of Browning, too.

> Bluish 'mid the burning water, full in face
>   Trafalgar lay;
>
> In the dimmest North-East distance dawn'd
>   Gibraltar grand and gray
> — from 'Home-Thoughts, from the Sea' by Robert
> Browning

To Shackleton, Browning of all the 19th century poets best expressed the mystery of existence. It was as if man's role on Earth was to demonstrate faith, courage and endurance, and no poet ever met the riddle of the universe with a more radiant response than Browning. At least that is how English author and journalist Harold Begbie, who wrote *Shackleton, A Memory* (1922), interpreted the polar explorer's reading of Browning.[3]

During weeks at sea Shackleton made up for his less-than-

attentive time at Dulwich by devouring great works of literature —
Shakespeare, Dickens, Longfellow — and specialist works as well,
including Darwin's 1859 classic, *On the Origin of Species*. Then,
in 1899, Shackleton's Merchant Navy career took a new turn.
He joined the Union Castle Line, a prestigious British shipping
company running passengers and cargo to and from southern
Africa. When the South African War erupted in October of that
year, the liners carried British troops from Southampton to Cape
Town. From two voyages in the *Tintagel Castle* he and the ship's
surgeon, with entrepreneurial vision, put together a 60-page
souvenir book. It was the young officer's first foray into the world
of publishing.[4] Printed and distributed by the co-authors and co-
publishers, the little book sold out on subscription and turned a
profit. A specially bound copy was presented to Queen Victoria;
another was inscribed: 'E. to E. July 1900 — The First Fruits'.
Emily was clearly in his sights. So was an emerging opportunity to
explore Antarctica.

Shackleton made several more voyages to Cape Town in Union
Castle liners before signing off from the merchant service in March
1901 — his final discharge. He was 27. The Royal Geographical
Society and Royal Society were putting together a polar expedition
and he wanted badly to be a part of it.

3 —
MALT MATURING

Too far north by several degrees of latitude for vineyards to flourish, the coastal land around Inverness and the neighbouring Speyside district is where barley grows richly, and arguably best, in Scotland. Across the maritime humps and hollows of these downlands and over much of the Black Isle near Inverness the golden grain ripens in the long summer evenings. Towards the higher country inland, misty glens and open expanses of heather keep company with rippling, salmon-run rivers that drain water from the Cairngorm and Grampian Mountains into the Moray Firth and the North Sea.

In the 1890s, the decade of Shackleton's Merchant Navy service, whisky distilling boomed in Speyside. Twenty-one new distilleries were commissioned during the decade across the district, on either side of the River Spey but mainly around the towns of Elgin, Rothes and Keith. It was an unprecedented expansion, an industrial blossoming. The coastal barley belt facing the Moray Firth was its anchor and its nourishment — that and the mountain-pure water tumbling through the district. Speyside labels have been at the forefront of the Scotch whisky industry ever since.

Barley field near Inverness.
DR JULIAN PAREN

Far back in time, barley had been the mainstay of the ale industry; its role in whisky production represented a new use.[5]

Take a harvest of the finest barley, steep it in water and spread it under cover to sprout for about a week. Germination and starch/sugar levels are carefully controlled by the dry heat of the kilning process, in which harvested peat is the traditional fuel. Peat imparts a range of flavours and aromas to the grain and thus to the whisky — flavours and aromas that vary according to the peat's plant-matter origins. The next stage, mashing, involves fermentation, the addition of yeast and the transformation of starch into fermentable sugars. Then comes the running of the resulting 'wash' through tall copper pot-stills, more than once, and boiling to vaporise and condense the spirit. Further distilling increases the alcohol content to around 70 per cent by volume, at which point the 'new-make' spirit is ready to be transferred to oak casks to mature.

The Glen Mhor distillery was set up in 1892 at Inverness. The site was strategic. Beside it was a water source, the Caledonian Canal, on the main road south from Inverness.[6] James Mackinlay headed the project in partnership with John Birnie from the nearby Glen Albyn distillery. Producing its first whisky in 1894, Glen Mhor was destined to ride the region's whisky wave in both blended whiskies and single malts. James's father, Charles Mackinlay, had established Chas. Mackinlay & Co. at Leith, north of Edinburgh, in 1847 after working for years for other whisky firms, and James's younger brother, Charles, was a second-generation partner. Charles junior managed the Glen Mhor distillery until he died in 1896, aged 48, just as the company was working on a Highland Malt Whisky line. Through the decades the Mackinlays collaborated with other notable names in the Scotch business

The Glen Mhor distillery, Inverness.
MACKINLAY FAMILY COLLECTION

— Dewar, Walker, Usher, Buchanan. Charles Mackinlay, the founder, was regarded as an early exponent of blended whiskies. It is thought that he might have latched on to the concept through working as an apprentice in the 1830s for tea merchants Walker & Hunter, who knew all about blends, and who were also wine and spirit dealers.

In the 1870s, the Mackinlay premises at Leith were expanded. A new bonded warehouse was erected and new blending and bottling equipment installed to increase production for the London market. In England in the 1880s, Scotch had an image problem. It was considered less suave, less well bred than, say, brandy or cognac. You really only drank whisky during vigorous, manly outdoor recreation, such as hunting deer or game birds, or salmon fishing on a wild river up north. Or if you were lower-class with unsophisticated tastes. It was generally not the drink to be offered in London drawing rooms, where brandy was the tipple of choice. The Shackleton drawing room at Sydenham, for moral and religious reasons, was patently off limits to whisky.

In 1879, founder Charles Mackinlay appointed the enterprising Canadian-born John Buchanan as the Mackinlay agent in London, and followed this up by making James, his elder son, the company's London director in 1885. Mackinlay's Vatted Old Benvorlich whisky was one of the first blended whiskies on the London market. James Mackinlay and John Buchanan worked wonders for the company, lifting its profile and sales through innovative advertising and personal contact. Mackinlay's won a contract to supply the House of Commons. They had penetrated the corridors of power.

By the late 1890s the Glen Mhor distillery was in continuous operation and building its stocks of malt whisky in casks. It tapped into the local barley crop and drew water from the Caledonian Canal, which in turn was supplied by the River Ness and its source to the south, Loch Ness. A cold, deep, glacial lake, Loch Ness occupies a stretch of Scotland's Great Glen, a fault-controlled rift in the Earth's crust angling southwest through Scotland, straight as a die, from the North Sea to the North Atlantic. Among the Scottish lochs, Ness, 37 kilometres long, is second only to Loch Lomond in length and surface area. For much of the year its surface waters are cold, below 10 degrees Celsius, clear and biologically limited, properties typical of a mountain lake. Human sewage discharges into the loch in modern times have periodically compromised its quality, but around the turn of the 20th century, when Glen Mhor was producing its first whiskies, the Ness waters were close to pristine. Pure water, pure whisky.[7]

There was one major ingredient that Mackinlay's decided in the 1890s to source from elsewhere: peat. The peat deposits on Dava Moor, inland from Nairn in the Speyside district, were available, but the Orkney Islands, off the north coast of mainland Scotland at latitude 59 degrees north and largely treeless, produced peats of unique character. When it came to whiskies, Orkney peat was a world apart from the peats of Islay or Jura, Speyside or Aberdeenshire, most of which had origins more woody.[8]

The Isle of Eday, slim, salty centrepiece of the Orkney archipelago, was where Mackinlay's sourced peat in the mid-1890s. The deposits there, overlying the mudstone bedrock, were so dark the locals called the hand-cut sods 'inkies'. The peat at the northern end of Eday was denser. It burnt more fiercely. Glen Mhor and its sister distillery, Glen Albyn, both imported shipments of Eday peat, which was landed at Morangie Beach to the north of Invergordon from small cargo vessels that would pick their days to cross the tempestuous strait of the Pentland Firth. The main island of Orkney was also a major producer and exporter of peat. A consignment was shipped to Australia in 1893.

So the kilns of Glen Mhor burned bright and aromatic with Eday peat, which conveyed its smokiness and salt to the barley grains and onward into the malt and new-make spirit. A maltster might choose to enhance flavour by adding clumps of heather to the fuel. When that happened the blue-grey smoke typical of peat would contain wisps of other colours, depending on what kind of heather was chosen.

For the maturing process, Mackinlay's acquired a line of 50-gallon barrels made of American white oak that had been used for sherry or bourbon production. Filled with new-make spirit and sealed, the barrels were stored three layers high in the warehouses of Glen Mhor for the long sleep of maturation. They lay there behind stone walls on wooden runners above an earth floor, the air continuously cool and damp. Physically and chemically, American oak was known to be the best pillow for the clear spirit. The spirit slept soundly, and in the dark stillness it drew colour and certain flavours from the oak timber — among them, toastiness, vanilla and coconut. The oak was also a skin through which the spirit expelled nasty sulphur compounds. It lost a little volume each year, too. Through evaporation a barrel could lose up to two per cent in 12 months, a phenomenon distillers call the Angels' Share. It was a gift to the heavens. Reducing like a gourmet sauce slowly gaining character on low heat, the spirit submits to the forces, charm and flavour enhancement that is the process of maturation in oak.

Market forces were on the minds of the Mackinlay directors in the 1890s as the whisky industry went on a charm offensive through smart advertising, new products and racy new names.

A worked peat bank in Orkney.
NEVILLE PEAT

Exports lifted. Scotch began to acquire pedigree status. The United States was a promising market, but trading improved as well with distant parts of the empire: the old colonies of India, Australia and New Zealand.

With one eye on what was maturing in their banks of oak barrels and the other eye on the market, the principals of Chas. Mackinlay & Co. were no doubt feeling happy with their place in the world of whisky as a new century dawned.

4 —
AN 'INVALID' IN ANTARCTICA

T he Queen is dead; long live the King!' As Shackleton was rounding
out his career in the Merchant Navy on the Cape Town run in
early 1901, the Victorian era drew to a close. Victoria, Queen-
Empress since her 19th year, not quite five feet tall yet a towering
world figure, became very frail and bed-ridden as 1900 rolled into
1901. On 22 January she slipped away at the age of 82. No monarch in
history had ruled for as long, 64 years. Her son and heir the Duke of
York, sporting a grey beard, was crowned King Edward VII.

The advent of the Edwardian era coincided with a new start for
Shackleton. The British National Antarctic Expedition of 1901–
04, Britain's first official Antarctic exploration in 60 years, was
masterminded not by the Admiralty but by the Royal Geographical
Society and Royal Society. Naval officers, nonetheless, were
to make up all but two of the 11-strong officer complement and
the bulk of the 36 crew. Two officers from the merchant service
were recruited, Shackleton one of them. He scraped in through
the intervention of a Royal Geographical Society contact, who
recommended him.

An early
newspaper
advertisement
for Mackinlay's
whisky.
MACKINLAY FAMILY
COLLECTION

Officially a sub-lieutenant in the Royal Naval Reserve, Shackleton gained the rank of third lieutenant on the *Discovery*, the expedition's Scottish-built and specially equipped vessel, and had the role of stores officer. It was his job to supervise the cargo handling and activity in the holds, and account for the stores and provisions, including all the food and sledging rations. Wardroom catering was another responsibility, as was sea-water analysis, a routine line of work. A junior lieutenant's role (Charles Royds and Michael Barne were his seniors, both Royal Navy) would not have bothered Shackleton; the prospect of polar adventure was enough to put a spring in his step and an added sparkle in his bright, slate-blue eyes.

Leading the expedition was a Royal Navy lieutenant, Robert Falcon Scott, promoted to commander. He was 33, six years older than Shackleton. *Discovery* left the London Docks on 31 July 1901, bound for New Zealand and the Ross Sea sector of Antarctica, which had been claimed by Britain. Belgian-born physicist Louis Bernacchi was the only expedition member with previous Antarctic experience. A brand-new ship, 52 metres long, *Discovery* was designed for ice work. With an ironclad bow for ramming sea ice, she could be iced in over winter, just like *Belgica*, with her propeller and rudder lifted out of harm's way. A coal-fired steam engine and barque-rigged sails provided propulsion.

Five months after leaving England *Discovery* made landfall in Antarctica, and soon Shackleton and other officers were trying out a manned balloon on a massive ice shelf, the Great Ice Barrier, which James Clark Ross had discovered during a British exploring expedition in 1841. Land sighted to the west was promptly named King Edward VII Land. McMurdo Sound, on the eastern side of the ice shelf, became their destination, and at the southern tip of Ross

Island, Scott ordered the erection of the expedition's hut. For meals and accommodation, though, *Discovery* continued to serve as the expedition base, for the hut was not well insulated. Bizarrely, it had the appearance of an Australian outback bungalow. It had a wide verandah on all four sides, as if in defence of solar heat.

The expedition's scientists, including zoologist Edward Wilson, who was also the expedition artist and a doctor, went about their work till the onset of winter shut down most activity. Wilson and Shackleton became 'inseparable friends', collaborating on a number of projects, including the setting up of a weather station on Crater Hill, close to Hut Point and Winter Quarters Bay. First Lieutenant Royds RN also found Shackleton 'good company' and admired his story-telling talent, although commented that the merchant man was 'both fore and aft' — a reference to Shackleton's egalitarian outlook and his reluctance to express officer-class superiority.

The third lieutenant, being in charge of stores, had plenty to do with the able seamen (ABs) on board, and with one AB in particular, Frank Wild, he became friendly. Wild, a Yorkshireman, had joined the Royal Navy from the merchant service, seeking new horizons. Like Shackleton, he was incurably adventurous. Wild's strength and tirelessness, despite his short stature (5 feet 4½ inches) and slight build, impressed Shackleton. It may have helped cement a bond between them, too, that Wild, like Shackleton, hailed from a religious and teetotal family.

During the 1902 winter Shackleton amused himself and others by producing a magazine, *The South Polar Times*, which took a leaf out of similar efforts at printed entertainment that had been produced on North Pole expeditions. *The South Polar Times* doubled as a diary of events and a showcase for creative prose, poetry and artwork, signed or anonymous. Shackleton rounded up contributions with his usual ebullience, and typed and edited them. Wilson's artwork was exquisite. His drawings were precise; his watercolours conveyed hues no outsider would have thought possible in a white desert.

Spring and the return of the sun came soon enough. It was time for sledging, the first long sledge journeys undertaken in Antarctica. Shackleton was an early and eager participant, although like Scott and the other officers he regarded the sled dogs that accompanied *Discovery* more as pets and recreational company than as draught animals. Manhauling was really the way to go, although as the officer in charge of the dogs he had a duty to exercise them and to try them out on journeys across the ice shelf and sea ice.

From the outset and for patriotic reasons — the old flag of empire and the new king — the expedition had envisaged making an assault on the South Pole through the 1901–02 summer. Scott devised a plan. He would lead it. There would be a support party to lay depots, but for the push to the Pole he would take just two others: Wilson and Shackleton. Scott recognised Shackleton's barrel-chested strength and vigour, developed from his sailor days. Wilson had also proved himself in the field, and his medical skills were valuable. They would take dogs but did not have high expectations of them. Scurvy was their main concern. Shackleton had come to believe that long expeditions into the unknown could overcome scurvy through eating fresh meat.

On 2 November, they set out south across the Barrier, not knowing how far it would take them towards the Pole. This was the mysterious unknown Shackleton had dreamed about, and three months of it lay ahead. The three explorers had each written a farewell letter to their loved ones, with Shackleton's addressed to 'my own dear Heart', Emily Dorman, to be opened only if he

failed to return. He poured out his deep love for her.

Across the ice shelf they travelled, the dogs doing most of the hauling. None of the trio could ski with confidence and the rough surface did not instil any. Towards the end of November the support party turned back. The Pole Party pushed on, relaying loads ahead to make depots for their return trip. Conditions on the ice shelf were no smoother going into December: the going was mostly flat but armed with jagged sastrugi ice and crevasses in places, and the adjacent mountain chain, which they would likely have to penetrate judging by the way it was cutting across ahead of them, looked formidable if not impassable. They weathered blizzards, fatigue and snow-blindness, with their eye pain relieved by a cocaine-laced compound slipped under the eyelids.

Then came signs of scurvy. On 21 December Wilson checked Shackleton's gums. They were 'decidedly angry-looking'. He informed Scott, and the two of them agreed to keep the news from Shackleton in the meantime. Three days later Scott's gums were affected and Wilson had a painful left eye. Frozen seal meat was all they relied on for fresh food. They celebrated Christmas doubtful about achieving the Pole, given they still had so far to go.

Shackleton, in charge of sledging rations, did his best to make the Christmas meals a highlight. Breakfast was a large helping of seal liver fried in bacon and pemmican fat, and a generous spoonful of jam to follow. Lunch was hot cocoa and milk biscuits. In the evening, as a treat, Shackleton produced small pieces of bacon that he had 'hoarded religiously' and served them up inside their tent of green canvas followed by the usual fare, boiled up pemmican hoosh with biscuits. Surprise, surprise, he also presented Scott and Wilson with a six-ounce plum pudding, the size of a cricket ball, that he had stowed in a spare sock. Then, after heating it up in a pot of cocoa and dousing it with emergency brandy, he set fire to the dessert with a rush of Christmas spirit and a sprig of holly, the worse for wear and age. Following days on starvation rations, this meal was one to remember.

What he really would have liked to eat that day was noted in his diary under the heading 'Desire': 'Duck crisp fried bread with salt and pepper; Thick bread soaked in golden syrup; Porterhouse steak and onions with plenty gravy; Huge salad of fruit, and also green stuff.' His dream menu extended to a sirloin of beef with brown crisp fat and, for sweets, a pile of pastry jam tarts attended by a bowl of cream.

The grim fact was, though, they were running short of food and fuel, and their dogs were dying and not able to pull any longer. The dead ones were fed to the living.

On 28 December, Scott wrote: 'We have almost shot our bolt.' They knew they must turn back soon to survive. Two days later, in murky weather, they did, still on the ice shelf and with the mountains still a bulwark to progress directly south. They realised now that a departure in the first week of November was at least a month too late for an expedition on foot to reach the Pole. Put it down to pioneering experience.

Their Farthest South, where no one had ventured before, was, as Scott recorded, 'between 82.16 S and 82.17 S'. They were opposite a broad embayment, to be named Shackleton Inlet, with impressive Mount Markham (4350 metres), named after the expedition sponsor-organiser Sir Clements Markham, president of the Royal Geographical Society, looming in the distance. From here it was a long way to the Pole — they were only a little over a third of the way there. But they had turned none too soon.

The return trek was a wretched experience, marked by

starvation, sickness and weakness of a kind the trio had never known. By 14 January, Shackleton's condition became a major concern. His gums were dark and swollen. Worse, he gasped for breath as coughing fits took hold, and at times he spat blood. Reducing weight on the two sledges, the pitiful little party made for the next food depot with as much haste as they could muster. Their last two dogs were shot to put them out of their misery. Shackleton walked or skied where possible beside the sledges, unable to manhaul or work the makeshift canvas sails, but he never complained about his illness. It worsened on 29 January with a restless night of coughing and heavy breathing. The next day, for a couple of hours, he accepted a ride on one of the sledges.

Now, with Ross Island in sight, the sun out and no wind, Shackleton staged a recovery. Wrote Scott: 'For two days the weather has been glorious, and has a wonderful effect on our invalid, who certainly has great recuperative powers.' They found themselves on a highway of sledge and ski tracks that led back to the imprisoned *Discovery* and Hut Point, where they found a welcoming feast and the comfort of their bunks. They had marched for 93 days. Not only had the National Antarctic Expedition's pitch at the Pole come up well short, Shackleton's participation would also be shortened.

As planned, the vessel *Morning* arrived from New Zealand, bringing fresh supplies to enable Scott's party to spend a second winter — and a third winter, if necessary — based in McMurdo Sound. The festive dinner aboard *Discovery* to welcome *Morning's* officers included 'skua gull' for entrée following by their one and only turkey. It was, as Scott wrote, 'a right merry night', although he did not specify what was available in the way of strong drink.

Shackleton was in no mood to celebrate when he was presented soon afterwards with Scott's decision to invalid him home. That decision was made with advice from the expedition's doctors. Later Scott would say that Shackleton had been 'forced to leave us by ill health'.[9] On the surface, it seemed that Scott believed Shackleton's health might have suffered from a second winter in Antarctica. But were there other factors, not the least a personality clash? Scott would later express 'regret' for having sent Shackleton home as the expedition team had lost an officer 'always brimful of enthusiasm and good fellowship' and a 'marvel of intelligent energy'.

On the eve of *Morning*'s departure for New Zealand, sea ice still trapped *Discovery* off Hut Point. A grand farewell party was hosted aboard *Morning* at the McMurdo Sound ice edge. The day before, Shackleton had reluctantly placed his luggage on the sledges heading over to *Morning*, accompanied by several others from *Discovery* who were also going home. After a splendid dinner in the wardroom, the party continued around the ship's piano. The air became thick with tobacco smoke and the songs rang out well into the small hours. Shackleton was hardly happy to be leaving when there was so much polar exploring to do, but he was buoyed by the thought of returning to England and his beloved Emily, and he partied till 3 a.m. Wild, who was staying with *Discovery*, and another seaman were among the last to call it a night. The party-goers from *Discovery* were hardly asleep before they had to get up again and make their way back across the sea ice. Wild and his mess-deck friend had to be tied to their sledge for safety.

As *Morning* slipped through the new frazil ice forming a soupy layer near the sea's surface, a southerly breeze astern and black sky ahead, Shackleton kept his thoughts about leaving largely to himself. It was as if he knew, as certainly as the sea ice receded and advanced over McMurdo Sound year in, year out, that he would be back.

5 —
SHACKLETON'S MEN

O nce back in England, Shackleton put his 'intelligent energy' to good use. Whether Scott would have approved of his presenting lectures and writing feature articles about the National Antarctic Expedition's first year of achievements is debatable, but he went ahead with publicising the expedition's efforts anyway, especially the Farthest South push for the Pole. That journey would rate as epic even before Scott himself could tell London audiences as much.

Journalism became Shackleton's first paid shore job. In the autumn of 1903, perhaps buoyed by his experience of editing *The South Polar Times*, he joined the *Royal Magazine* as a sub-editor. This monthly literary publication, a periodical in the stable of publishing magnate Sir Arthur Pearson, no doubt appealed to Shackleton's literary bent if not to his interest in new ventures. Just five years old, it was in the process of establishing itself.

But he lasted just a few months. As the magazine's editor opined about his polar recruit, 'office work was out of his line altogether'. Shackleton's enthusiasm never waned; he just needed to find his niche.

A lecture Shackleton presented in Edinburgh for the Royal Scottish Geographical Society led to his taking on paid employment with the society in January 1904, as its secretary. Through his organisational skills and his winning public persona, he put the society on a sounder footing and boosted its membership.

His private life was moving swiftly, too. Since his return to England, Emily Dorman had provided romance and a link back into London society and its cultural mores, including the theatre and art exhibitions. After leaving London journalism he bought a house on the outskirts of Edinburgh and proudly showed it off to Emily, his 'darling Sweeteyes'. On 9 April they were married in London, at Christ Church, Westminster, and made their home in Edinburgh.

Yet Antarctica was never far away from Shackleton's thoughts. After the triumphant return of *Discovery* in September 1904 his lecture engagements continued. Both he and Scott were on the road speaking about the National Antarctic Expedition's feats, and both received the Polar Medal from the King as reward for distinguished service in Antarctica. Even at the time he became a father for the first time — a son, Raymond, was born in February 1905 — he wrote to a friend: 'What I would give to be out there again doing the job and this time really on the road to the Pole.'

He was certainly restless. Resigning from the Royal Scottish Geographical Society in January 1905 but staying on in Edinburgh, he cast around for work in new settings, preferably ones that could generate a fortune if not fame. He dabbled in a cigarette retail business and later proposed a bizarre and somewhat doomed plan to transport battalions of Russian troops by sea from the Far East. Through 1905, he spent a number of months with no work at all. His best prospects appeared to be with a Glasgow industrialist,

William Beardmore, who was making a fortune in shipbuilding and steelworks on the Clyde. London born, Beardmore had moved at the age of five to Glasgow, where his father had co-founded a steel mill. With links to Dulwich College, he and Shackleton shared some common ground. They had met in Edinburgh while Shackleton was revitalising the Geographical Society. Beardmore recognised the younger man's drive and ambition, and may have thought him a prospect for reviving the Arrol-Johnston motor works, a car company newly acquired by Beardmore.

In the event, Shackleton became secretary of the company's technical committee and also took on a kind of public relations role in the Beardmore industrial empire. In this latter role he travelled around impressing the company's business friends or potential clients, smartly turned out in collar and tie and three-piece suit, with his dark hair stylishly parted in the centre. He also took part in brainstorming ideas for industrial initiatives. At the time he was still residing in Edinburgh and commuted by train to the Glasgow office.

For a time in 1906, Shackleton let his moneymaking and polar ambitions take a back seat to political moves. He joined the Liberal-Unionist Party and stood as a candidate for Dundee in the 1906 general election, only to be roundly defeated, coming fourth out of five candidates. If the voters wanted to see more Pole than politics from him in the future, they would not be disappointed.

In 1906, too, he put together a four-page proposal, in the form of a printed pamphlet, for an expedition to 'the Ross Quadrant of the Antarctic with a view to reaching the Geographical South Pole and the Magnetic South Pole'. He would take ponies, dogs and, yes, a specially designed motor vehicle. He envisaged the motor vehicle steadily hauling a train of 10 sledges towards the Geographic South Pole, and on the way back it would explore outlying areas east and west of the Pole route. Although he wanted to lead a private expedition, it would be British through and through. It would plant a Union Jack at the Pole. It would erase Terra Incognita, and fame would follow.

The plan brimmed with confidence, but who would fund it? Shackleton knew that financing Antarctic expeditions was not easy and, as he told an associate, he was 'rather more than ordinarily handicapped' — likely a reference to a string of refusals he had received from men of wealth and influence.

In the end, his employer became his main patron. William Beardmore agreed to guarantee a bank loan to the tune of £7,000 — a substantial lump sum, the kind of money that could lever additional support. Additional support came in the form of personal loans and a rough guess of what a book, magazine and newspaper articles, and illustrated lectures could bring in after the expedition — £30,000. Shackleton broke the news of his windfall and his firming polar plans to his wife shortly after she had given birth to Cecily, their second child, in December 1906.[10] She did not stand in the way.

Two months later, in February 1907, her husband made his plans public in a newspaper announcement and followed this up in more detail in the March edition of the *Geographical Journal*. A shore party of 'nine or twelve men' would undertake three separate sledging journeys. The most important would try to reach the Geographic South Pole. Another sledging team would seek the Magnetic South Pole, and the third would explore King Edward VII Land east of the Great Ice Barrier. A scientific programme would be carried out throughout the expedition. Its predecessor, the National Antarctic Expedition of 1901–04, had been sponsored by two venerable and learned organisations with the backing of the Admiralty and a naval way of doing things. The 1907 expedition would be a smaller venture, which he would organise and lead. It acquired a proud and punchy title, the British Antarctic Expedition. Government involvement would be minimal.

Shackleton originally intended using Scott's base in McMurdo Sound, the Discovery Hut at Hut Point, but changed his mind after Scott, promoted to captain since returning to Royal Navy duties, responded tersely to that scenario. McMurdo Sound was 'primarily mine', Scott argued. He claimed, as he put it, 'a sort of right to my own fieldwork', and intended leading a second expedition there in a year or two.

Shackleton described the revelation of another Scott-led national expedition as 'staggering news', but took the hint about occupation rights in respect of Discovery Hut. He would instead aim to set up a base on King Edward VII Land and lead a Pole party across the Barrier well clear of the rugged backbone of mountains. Scott's plans did not necessarily conflict with his own, but they did stymie his hopes of recruiting National Antarctic Expedition expertise. One after another, starting with Edward Wilson, Scott's men — officers and scientists — rejected Shackleton's feelers. He had to widen his search for men who would make up the shore party. At the same time, he had to arrange a ship, a prefabricated base hut, and all the food, fuel and provisions to last a year at least. When it came to the stores, he had no qualms, having been in charge of them on the previous British expedition. This time he could be innovative and use his powers of persuasion like never before.

First, the expedition needed a headquarters. A furnished office upstairs at 9 Regent Street, Waterloo Place, was chosen, right in the middle of an avenue of five- and six-storey stone buildings in the heart of Edwardian London's white-collar precinct, the hub of the illustrious St James–Soho–Mayfair triangle. This concrete jungle was about as far away, physically and naturally, from the ice expanses of Antarctica as you could get. On the other hand, it was a brisk 20-minute walk through St James Park to Big Ben and the Houses of Parliament, where there were people of influence. They might be useful. Picture, then, Shackleton at his new place of work . . .

The British Antarctic Expedition office is a small, lean enterprise. There is a manager, Alfred Reid, whom Shackleton has recruited on the strength of his efficiency and experience with previous polar expeditions, and an office assistant who is the secretary and courier. Secretarial backup, in the form of a typing agency, occupies the same building — the same floor, in fact. A telephone connects the expedition leader with the outside world. In Regent Street, men in bowler hats (and an occasional top hat) ride in open-topped buses. Renault taxis with newfangled meters have all but displaced horse-drawn hansom cabs. On the political front, always of interest to Shackleton, the Women's Suffrage Movement is planning a traffic-stopping demonstration in nearby Trafalgar Square.

One of the first requirements for this new Antarctic venture is a supply of letterhead. An order form, printed from the main run of letterhead, carries the lines:

> Messrs . . . .
> Please put in hand the following goods for the above
> Expedition for delivery in London in . . . next:

A 2012 view of the Regent Street, London, office block that housed the 1907 British Antarctic Expedition.
NEVILLE PEAT

The office is soon a receiving house for all manner of provisions and equipment that Shackleton has sourced and costed even before the expedition is made public. He opts for 'the best of everything'.

One of his ideas is to use space at 9 Regent Street to display examples of the goods and gear he and the mustachioed Reid will order over the coming months — show them off to friends and supporters of the expedition, and potential sponsors. It is good public relations, and the smallest donations are welcome. Visitors will marvel at the sledges, tents, cooking apparatus, scientific instruments and the special foods for sledging, including the Plasmon biscuits enriched with dried milk and vitamins. All this is state-of-the-art provender for polar work, much of it donated. Shackleton and Reid have been meeting the heads of businesses supplying the expedition, negotiating discounts and gratis deals. (What he loves about the office set-up and the procurement process is that he is 'not hampered by committees of any sort'. There is no higher authority, no reference group, no steering committee. He is the boss.)

But above all when it comes to organising this expedition, Shackleton wants to personally select the men who will help him attain the Pole. Some will come to the office to be interviewed, some he will go out of his way to contact and visit. A few he will simply bump into. He wants 11 good men and true.

An early recruit is Ernest Joyce, who was an able seaman on the Discovery expedition. His signing up for the British Antarctic Expedition is an example of Shackleton opportunism at its flukiest. Shackleton is looking out the window of his office one day when a bus passes. On its open upper deck he spots the familiar face of Joyce and his thick mop of hair. Joyce impressed the officers under Scott for his sledging expertise and resilience in the field. At once, Shackleton calls on his office assistant to run after the bus, intercept Joyce and bring him back to the office. Joyce is pleasantly surprised to be offered another trip to Antarctica. He can look after the dogs as well as the sledges, says Shackleton. Joyce, a year older than the expedition leader, is still a naval rating but tells his new-found leader he will make himself available by resigning from the Royal Navy.

Although the Joyce sign-up was swift and effortless, others took time. Months passed before the shore party had a substantial look to it. He received more than 400 applications and carefully sifted through them, looking for men after his own heart — strong of mind and body, for sure, but also adventurous, unafraid to take risks, and solidly optimistic. There was another attribute, which he wrote about: 'They must be able to live together in harmony for a long period without outside communication, and it must be remembered that the men whose desires lead them to the untrodden paths of the world have generally marked individuality.'

Another expedition member recruited early on was Lieutenant Jameson Boyd Adams. Like Shackleton, he had a background in the Merchant Navy and the Royal Naval Reserve. Solidly built, Adams had met Shackleton in Scotland the previous summer, learnt of the yet-to-be-revealed shot at the Pole and asked if he could join the shore party. By telegram in early 1907 Shackleton made the offer. Adams accepted. He would be named second-in-command, aged 27.

Another recruit whom Shackleton had met in 1906 was a young baronet, Sir Philip Brocklehurst. Sir Philip was tall and strapping and in his 20th year in 1907, with romantic notions of polar travel. But he had means, with a family fortune behind him, and his mother readily agreed to contribute funds to the expedition. Intent on making himself useful, Sir Philip took courses in geology and surveying at Cambridge University.

Geological expertise was also recruited through Raymond Priestley, who was only nine months older than the baronet and halfway through his geological studies at University College, Bristol. He was puzzled about being chosen when he knew of at least a dozen honours graduates who wanted to go. But Shackleton, an astute judge of character, liked the conscientious look of Priestley and that, along with the prospect of sponsorship, was enough.

Shackleton's shore party would include only two members with Antarctic experience. The second, after Joyce, was Yorkshireman Frank Wild. Like Joyce, Wild, now a petty officer, had been a naval rating with *Discovery*, practical and keen in the field and an experienced sledging hand. Despite his slight build he seemed impervious to cold. Ten months older than Shackleton, Wild would also quit the Royal Navy and a decent naval pension for a life of adventure in cold places. Wild worked hard and played hard. Shackleton had observed first hand Wild's liking of strong drink, especially whisky, but did not hold that against him. Wild would look after the all-important stores.

Eric Marshall was enlisted as the expedition's senior surgeon. Tall, physically powerful and at times dogmatic, Marshall had just graduated in medicine from Cambridge University at the age of 27. At one point he had studied to be a Church of England minister, but finally chose medicine and practised as a surgeon at St Bartholomew's Hospital, London. He had met Shackleton at a house party in 1906, heard of the possibility of another Pole expedition and offered on the spot to contribute his services. He would take on map work and navigation as well as medical duties and photography. The assistant surgeon was a Scotsman from Argyllshire, Alistair Mackay, two years older than Marshall. He had been in some challenging situations — a naval surgeon for four years, a trooper in the South African War and a member of Baden-Powell's national police force in South Africa. The Manchurian ponies would be among his responsibilities on the Ice.

One of the most specialised recruits was a motor mechanic, Bernard Day, who had been working for William Beardmore's Arrol-Johnston Motor Company in Scotland. Day, aged 23, would be the mechanic and driver of the expedition car and the electrician at the base hut. Shackleton expected a lot from the car. It would have special adaptations for polar use. The mechanic was part of the Beardmore package because the car was experimental. It was going to undertake the first road test of a motor vehicle in Antarctic conditions. The cook's position was also full-time and it fell to a hotel chef, William Roberts, one of those who formally applied. Shackleton wanted his team well fed, and the 35-year-old Roberts got the nod both for his competence and his experience of working in various parts of the world. He liked a challenge overseas.

Although the expedition's scientific programme did not rank above its geographical aims, the studies in geology, biology, meteorology and oceanography were important in any Antarctic expedition, and Shackleton knew the scientific component would help sell the 1907 British Antarctic Expedition to sponsors. The appointment of principal biologist went to James Murray, one of the oldest members of the expedition at 42. Born in Glasgow and self-taught, he had studied microscopic life in the Scottish lochs and was keen to see what Antarctica had to offer.

The 11th position in the team, one of Shackleton's favourites, was that of expedition artist.

It would be the artist's job to put together a graphic record of expedition life in various media, complementing the photographic record that would be ensured by the rapid development in cameras and the art of photography. From the 30 applications for the job, Shackleton selected three contenders. He asked them all to report to his Regent Street office on a Saturday morning. One said he was busy and could not come till Monday, a second wanted to know if he could be certain of selection because he had to travel four hours. The third did not reply but showed up at the office, dripping wet and dishevelled, just as Shackleton was leaving. The latecomer explained he had been on a walking tour in Cornwall and caught a train as soon as he could. He was sorry for his lateness but there had been several changes on the rail journey. 'I promptly engaged him,' Shackleton wrote later. He had hired George Marston, an art teacher who had studied at the Regent Street Polytechnic. His burly physique belied a playful sense of humour.

Marston's selection was vintage Shackleton, based on first impressions, a quick summing up and natural instinct. Including the leader the shore-party complement of 12 was now decided. There was a good balance of field and scientific expertise, and service roles. But Shackleton eventually came to realise that the expedition could benefit from bolstering the scientific side. Australia, on the way south, would provide the personnel.

6 —
THE ORDER

Quality and economy were imperatives in the purchase of provisions and equipment for the expedition. Shackleton wanted top-notch gear and the finest food and liquid refreshments, but he did not want to pay the earth for them. The two big items were a ship and a base building, both of which would have to face extreme conditions.

There were two ships in the running, both seal hunters. Shackleton coveted the Norwegian vessel *Bjorn*, 700 gross tons, three years old and with a price tag of £11,000. That last figure was the killer. Fast, powerful and specially designed for ice work, *Bjorn* was much too expensive, and with a crew of 50 probably too costly to operate. The second choice, *Nimrod*, was considerably older (40 years) and smaller (334 gross tons, 42 metres long), but rather less appealing to Shackleton on first inspection in the River Thames in June 1907. *Nimrod* needed refurbishment from stem to stern, including new masts and sails, and she stank of seal oil.

About to sail across the North Atlantic to the Newfoundland sealing grounds, *Nimrod* was purchased by Shackleton there and then for £5,000. This was closer to what he could afford. Her ice-rasped hull was constructed of oak, greenheart and ironbark, good strong timbers for manoeuvring through Arctic ice in search of seals, and her coal-fired engine could get her cruising at six knots. Counting the refit costs, she would gobble most of Beardmore's £7,000 guarantee.

Shackleton intended to rename his expedition ship *Endurance* in honour of his family motto, 'By endurance we conquer', but never managed to tackle the paperwork during the two-month refit that preceded her departure for New Zealand. *Nimrod* she remained, and during her transformation from sealer to Antarctic expedition ship Shackleton began to believe she could do the job. On the small side, yes, and somewhat underpowered; but he was not intending to use *Nimrod* for board and lodging through the 1908 winter in the way that Scott had used *Discovery* as the home of his expedition six years earlier. Shackleton simply wanted a ship that would deliver his team and their accoutrements to a base site and pick them up a year later.

The second major item on Shackleton's shopping list was a hut. He paid close attention to its design and specifications. He was careful about this because an overdesigned dwelling would not only cost more to build and take up more space in *Nimrod's* holds; it would also cost more to heat, and that meant carting more coal south. Humphreys Ltd, a construction firm in Knightsbridge at Hyde Park, a couple of kilometres from the expedition office, was engaged to prefabricate a 'timber-framed portable house', 33 feet (10 metres) long by 19 feet (5.8 metres) wide. Its height to the eaves would be eight feet (2.4 metres) and it would have a lean-to porch. Humphreys called themselves 'Iron Buildings Manufacturers' but they were confident working with wood — and keen, fit to burst. Shackleton supplied a drawing of his Antarctic hut on 17 May 1907, and the very same day Humphreys produced a four-page quotation for what they must have thought would be a piece of history. The specifications were detailed enough to suggest there had been prior discussions with the expedition leader about design and materials. The 20 clauses in the quote each dealt with an aspect of the building's construction or supply, starting with 'Wall Framing':

> *The Wall Framing to be constructed of good strong yellow deal [Scots pine, Pinus sylvestris], morticed and tenoned, so as to be easily taken down for re-erection, without injury to the structure, each joint to be plainly marked to facilitate re-erection.*

Insulating features were included: felt lining in the roof, slag wool between the outer and inner wall linings, double casement windows. No mention of floor insulation, but the finer details of ironmongery were covered: brass and iron fittings and the necessary bolts, screws and nails. Humphreys were efficient manufacturers. They guaranteed to have the hut erected and ready for inspection seven working days after confirmation of the order. And the quoted price for this unique piece of polar history? £154. A 20 per cent deposit was to be paid at the signing of the contract. Next to the cost of the expedition ship, the Nimrod Hut was a snip.

For specialised polar gear Shackleton and Reid travelled to Norway, where they ordered sledges, skis, reindeer-pelt sleeping bags, fur-lined boots, clothing, hats, gloves and equipment. They did not personally have to go everywhere to inspect necessary items because they had agents in Norway and other places — Manchuria, for example, in the case of the pony purchases, and Australia for certain scientific equipment.

London suppliers to the expedition, nonetheless, were many

Floor plan of the Nimrod Hut.
THE HEART OF THE ANTARCTIC 1909/
HAROLD LOWE COLLECTION

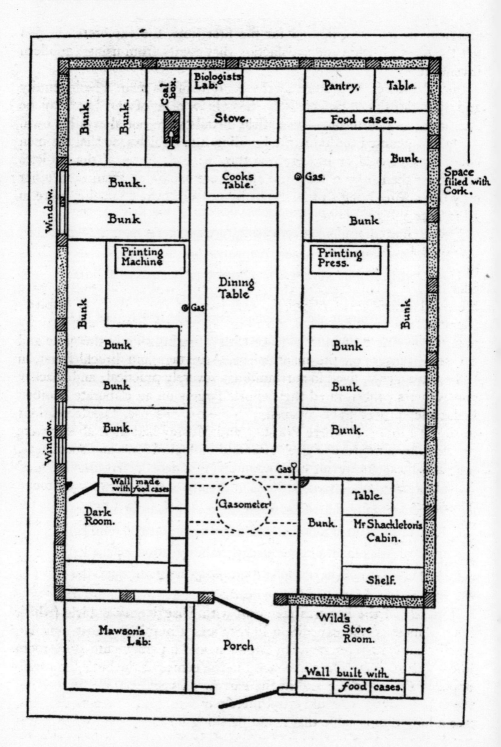

and varied. An important item was the coal range for the hut, which Smith & Wellstood supplied, together with flue and cowl, pokers, trays and spare rings. A lot of time, though, would be spent on sledging journeys beyond the comfort of the base hut, and these required an array of equipment, including tents, Nansen cookers, fuel, food bags, medical supplies, navigation and survey equipment, tools and climbing gear.

On the strength of the old Napoleonic saying that an army marches on its stomach, Shackleton decided his platoon would be well fed. He felt variety was important and the food had to be 'wholesome and nourishing in the highest degree possible'. If the shopping list ended up with some lavish items, so be it. On his mind — at times it obsessed him — was the battle he had had with scurvy on the Discovery expedition. His expedition ended up with 150 items of food in manufactured form — meats, fish, poultry, soups, cereals, jams, vegetables, fruit, spices, pickles, egg products, biscuits, puddings, confectionery, soft-drink mixes. They were a mixture of purchased, discounted and donated items. Donor companies included some well-known names — Colman, Bird, Rowntree, Lipton. Other major suppliers were Heinz, Quaker, McDoddies, Moir, Hartley, Nestlé. Among the larger items loaded in London: 14,000 lb (6 tonnes) flour; 1600 lb (726 kg) of finest York hams; 1500 lb (680 kg) granulated sugar; 1500 lb (680 kg) oatmeal; 1043 lb (473 kg) dried haricot beans; 1000 lb (454 kg) cocoa; 540 lb (245 kg) golden syrup; 2400 tins of soup; 450 tins of baked beans; 380 lb (172 kg) gooseberry jam; 300 bottles of lime juice. In New Zealand, Shackleton reckoned on loading dairy products, among the world's finest, and other fresh produce.

The food, in all its different packaging, was a logistical nightmare. Shackleton had a novel solution, a modular approach.

His brainwave might have come from his experience as a stores officer in the Merchant Navy and the cargo-handling efficiencies he might have contemplated but never had the opportunity to apply. What he came up with was a packing case made of venesta boards, a three-layer plywood that was light, strong and weatherproof. All cases were the same size, with a footprint of 30 inches (76 cm) by 15 inches (38 cm). They were a handy size to manhandle, and the venesta reduced *Nimrod*'s total loaded weight by a little over four tonnes. Empty, they would double as partitioning, shelving or seating in his Antarctic hut. His venesta invention was a coup.

Among the small mountain of consumables ordered or donated for the expedition, there were some he did not plan on repacking into the standard venesta model. These held liquor, with their bottles individually and specially packaged for sea travel.

The day before he sought a quote for the expedition hut, Ernest Shackleton signed off an order for 25 cases of whisky. Ten years earlier, enjoying the company of the elder son back home on shore leave, the family of Henry and Henrietta Shackleton could not have envisaged Ernest, at one time an ardent Band of Hope advocate, requesting 300 bottles of the kind of strong drink he had grown up abhorring because of its deleterious social effects.

Now, in May 1907, under British Antarctic Expedition letterhead, here he was ordering a truckload of liquor, 43 cases all up, a heady mix — 25 cases of whisky, 12 of brandy and six of port. Shackleton knew that, cooped up in a small hut in the coldest place on earth, his men would turn to occasional partying to relieve the confinement and tedium. For all his dislike of alcohol beyond a rare celebratory drink, he must have felt the expedition would be an unhappy unit without it.

In any event, the popular idea of the time was that whisky and

BRITISH ANTARCTIC EXPEDITION, 1907

9 REGENT STREET
(Waterloo Place)
LONDON, S.W.

16 May 1907

Messrs. Chas Mackinlay & Leith

Please put in hand the following goods for the above
Expedition for delivery in London in 20th July next:

per Mr Thomson g 31 Crutched Friars
London EC

25 (twenty cases) Mackinlays
Whisky 10 years old Md Brand
at 28/- per case
under bond

12 cases Old Liqueur Brandy
" at 60/- under bond

6 cases Old Port—matured
in wood 48/— under bond

Free of all charges, Free on board
Ship London. less 5% discount—
for Cash.

E.H. Shackleton

Commander

The handwritten order for whisky,
brandy and port for the British
Antarctic Expedition 1907.

brandy had medicinal value. If you were cold, alcohol could warm you up, and a hot toddy was just the thing to combat the common cold. Everyone knew about the legendary search-and-rescue dogs in the Swiss and Italian Alps, the St Bernard breed in particular, that carried brandy in little barrels attached around their necks while searching for people buried in avalanches or injured in the mountains. At times of duress, whisky or brandy had uplifting powers.[11]

The 1907 Nimrod order, although appearing to be in the handwriting of manager Alfred Reid, was signed, no question, by Shackleton — *E. H. Shackleton, Commander*. Whether Shackleton or his manager shopped around for a good deal on liquor purchases is not known. What is known is that the British Antarctic Expedition (BAE) negotiated a '5% discount for Cash', which suggests a discussion beforehand between the expedition office and the supplier, Chas. Mackinlay & Co., of Edinburgh, about age and other attributes of the liquor.

A 10-year-old whisky was specified. It carried the label 'M L'. The initials stood for 'Malt Liqueur', marketing spin for a malt whisky at the time. The purchase price was 28 shillings a case or 2.33 shillings a bottle, minus the discount. The order was for 25 cases, although the spelt-out version inadvertently stated 'twenty'. The brandy and port order, per case and bottle, was rather more expensive — 12 cases of 'Old Liqueur Brandy' at 60 shillings a case and six cases of Old Port ('matured in wood') at 48 shillings a case. All three spirits were to be supplied 'under bond', which meant delivery on board the expedition ship free of customs charges.

Delivery was requested for 20 July, by which time *Nimrod* was expected to be shipshape and loading up for the voyage to Antarctica. Mackinlay's representative in London, James Thomson, was to be the intermediary.

No one alive can say whether Shackleton winced at the ordering of so much whisky. He knew full well what he was doing, and he might even have whispered something to Manager Reid about placing another order for '12 (twelve)' cases of the exact same whisky a year hence to accompany *Nimrod*'s relief voyage south to pick up the expedition.

Why Mackinlay's? For one thing, Shackleton must have known the label had age and an air of quality about it and that it had a considerable following in London. Mackinlay's Scotch had appeared on the London market during whisky's renaissance in the capital. For another, it was a whisky that swirled about the Houses of Parliament at Westminster. Surely that was top-hat-doffing endorsement.

7 —
WHISKY AND THE ICE

Scotch served on ice is not recommended by connoisseurs because the ice will deaden or diminish the whisky's flavour and character. A dash of water, yes; blocks of ice, no.

At the Mackinlay office in Leith, Edinburgh, Shackleton's order is received with delight, although its arrival is not entirely unforeseen. Who knows what jokes may have done the rounds about how their Scotch would soon be heading for an encounter with a block of ice (with a capital I) of continental proportions? Two years earlier the company had built a new bonded warehouse in Queen Charlotte Street, Leith; there are plans for more in the next few years.

The whisky is at hand in the Glen Mhor Distillery at Inverness. It has been maturing in oak barrels in dark warehouse spaces for varying periods, but the final blend will justify the '10-year-old' tag. The warehouse air is fractionally denser and more aromatic than the air outside because of the subtle evaporation of the Angels' Share from the great array of barrels. Mackinlay's must now blend and bottle what they will describe on the label as a

'Rare Old Highland Malt Whisky'. Uniquely, the label will carry the words, 'Specially prepared for the British Antarctic Expedition 1907 — Ship *Endurance*'.

What do they mean by 'specially prepared'? The whisky is a blend of malts of different ages and distillations but originating from the same distillery, Glen Mhor. Hence it can be called a single malt. The blender has sampling, nosing and tasting to do — to the uninitiated, a mysterious and puzzling vocation — followed by the careful vatting that precedes bottling. Others in the firm must organise the 300 bottles, order the labels and the packaging materials, and stamp 25 wooden crates made of pine timber with the company logo, the whisky's name and an alert red deer stag with a spreading rack of antlers. Each case holds a dozen bottles lying down in three layers, and each bottle is to be wrapped in tissue paper and, for protection in the lumpy Southern Ocean, a good handful of coarse straw tied up with raffia string. Then there is the long trip to London to organise, by sea. All of this must happen inside nine weeks.

A hint of the style of whisky the company might have in mind to supply the British Antarctic Expedition is contained in correspondence the previous year, when Charles Mackinlay, grandson of the founder, wrote to liquor wholesalers about Mackinlay's innovative line of 'Highland Malt' whiskies in production at Glen Mhor. The Inverness distillery was already producing such whiskies in 1906, and the handwritten letter to wholesalers indicated 'sufficient reserve in bond at the Distillery to guarantee uniformity of age and quality in the future'. Charles Mackinlay's carefully worded and engagingly polite pitch to the wholesalers conceded that Pure Highland Malt whiskies were 'as a rule too heavy and rich for ordinary consumption'; but Glen

Mhor was offering something out of the ordinary — 'a whisky, which, whilst retaining all the excellent properties that the Pot Still method of manufacture imparts, is light and silent enough for consumption as a single whisky'. At the time, there was a legal debate going on to define Scotch whisky. It had captured the attention of the daily press and was very much in the public gaze. Mackinlay's wanted to make sure it was ahead of the game, a brand leader.

In 1907, James Mackinlay, son of the founder, is still the company's main man. He was the one who had led Mackinlay's foray into the London market back in the 1870s and won an order from the House of Commons in 1875. The company's first London office was in Queen Victoria Street (by the 1920s it would be located in Waterloo Place, Shackleton's old stamping ground). The Mackinlay's brand commands a presence in central London through the Edwardian era. But times are changing. Talk continues about the need to sort out the confusion between Irish whiskey and Scotch and the associated shenanigans in production and marketing. A legal definition of Scotch will help.[12]

The Macklinlay's office, by 1907, is located at 31 Crutched Friars, downriver from Waterloo Place and close to the Tower of London. In charge of the office is James Thomson, who receives from the commander of the next British exploration of Antarctica his instructions on how the crates of liquor are to be marked. The 19 June letter is typed this time under a new letterhead that includes the expedition's telegraphic address ('ANTEXPEDI, LONDON'). Shackleton asks for the 43 cases of whisky, brandy and port to be marked with the name 'British Antarctic Expedition 1907' and numbered off 1733 to 1755.

In about a month the consignment will be on its way south.

8 —
VOYAGE TO
NEW ZEALAND

In May 1907, Mackinlay & Co. must have been told that the expedition ship's name would change to *Endurance*. So in good faith the label around the neck of each bottle declared the transporting vessel to be *Endurance*. *Nimrod*, however, was the name she still carried on 30 July, the day she cast off from the East India Dock and, with black smoke belching, steamed serenely down the River Thames. Shackleton was on board for the first few days only. He planned to travel more quickly to Australia and New Zealand by a scheduled liner once he had tied up organisational loose ends and seen to last-minute arrangements, including any sponsorship he could secure. To his brother-in-law, Herbert Dorman, the expedition solicitor, he left the task of banking late donations to the cause.

Nimrod, after calling the first night at Greenhithe, sailed for Torquay on England's south coast, her old schooner configuration converted to a barquentine rig. On the way, though, she was intercepted by an Admiralty tug, which passed a message to Shackleton requesting that *Nimrod* make for Cowes on the Isle

An artist's impression of King Edward VII and Queen Alexandra inspecting a sledge and other gear on *Nimrod*'s deck at Cowes, August 1907.
THE HEART OF THE ANTARCTIC

of Wight, where the might of the Royal Navy was assembled for a Naval Review by King Edward VII. The Solent roadstead off Cowes was crowded with about 200 warships — cruisers, battleships and other classes, great lines of them. King Edward, monarch for six years, and Queen Alexandra were aboard the 4000-ton *Victoria and Albert III*, which dwarfed *Nimrod* when the royal yacht approached her. A royal visit to *Nimrod* on the eve of her departure for Antarctica was a dream start. Not yet a major public figure, Shackleton knew this would greatly lift the expedition's profile and sponsorship potential.

The King and Queen were welcomed on board *Nimrod* together with a retinue of three princes, a princess and a duke, as well as several Royal Navy eminences. It was a stellar moment for the former Newfoundland sealing vessel and for Shackleton, too, who was invested with the Victorian Order (Fourth Class). Queen Alexandra came with a gift for the expedition leader — a British flag. An attached note read: 'May this Union Jack, which I entrust to your keeping, lead you safely to the South Pole.' The royals and their entourage were shown various pieces of polar equipment, including the hut's component parts, neatly packaged, and, uniquely for an Antarctic expedition, the modified car.

This was not the first time Their Majesties had farewelled an Antarctic expedition. Scott's Discovery expedition had received a royal send-off during Cowes Week — the same week, six years earlier. Scott had 'longed to get away from our country as quietly as possible'; Shackleton, on the other hand, treasured the publicity in *The Times* and other newspapers. His was a private expedition requiring a lot more sponsorship, whereas Scott, who had support from well-heeled British institutions, was better funded.

After Cowes came Torquay, the final port of call in England. It

Nimrod at Cowes in the first
week of August 1907, bound for
New Zealand and the Antarctic.
*QUEEN ALEXANDRA'S CHRISTMAS GIFT
BOOK 1908*

was something of an anticlimax, especially as the only members of the shore party still on board for the long haul around the Cape of Good Hope to New Zealand were biologist James Murray and naval surgeon Alistair Mackay, who had studied biology as well as medicine. The main group of eight expedition members — Adams, Day, Joyce, Marshall, Marston, Priestley, Roberts and Wild — were booked on the one-class emigrant ship *Runic* of the White Star Line, Shackleton's former employer. To save money, they were crammed into one small cabin, which cost just £19 per passenger. Shackleton might have regarded the straitened accommodation as a form of team-building. They had six weeks to get acquainted aboard RMS *Runic*, time enough to sort out bunkmates for when they reached the Antarctic.

They realised by now, too, that there was more glory than salary to be gained from this expedition. The 11th man, Brocklehurst, had the means to travel to New Zealand in style and comfort and booked his own passage aboard the liner *Omrah*, sailing from Marseilles. Shackleton was the last to leave England, at the end of October. He sailed to Australia with a fast liner, *India*, via the Suez Canal. In Australia he hoped to recruit two geologists and raise funds to pay for them. Finance was tight.

Nimrod, meanwhile, had called at Cape Town and was slogging her way across the South Indian Ocean in November. In any kind of sea she moved about a lot, rolling and pitching, especially if she had reduced sail aloft. James Murray reckoned *Nimrod* would roll even if she were in the British Museum. Mackay chipped in with his own humour in a shipboard magazine called *Antarctic Petrel*. It referred to drinking. 'Work is the ruin of the drinking classes. If whisky-drinking interferes with your work, give up your work.'

The two Scotsmen occupied a dungeon-like cabin aft called

the Scientists' Quarters (known later as 'Oyster Alley'). Despite the refit and spring-clean it still reeked of *Nimrod*'s sealing days. The pair coped with the boredom of weeks at sea by collecting marine life, including giant basking sharks, fish of weird and wonderful shape and colour, and an absorbing array of micro-organisms. Murray and Mackay were also expected to contribute to deckhand chores such as painting — 'we justified our existence,' Murray wrote — and they learnt the sailors' sea shanties, which Murray described as 'doggerel put to music, a way for sailors to overcome boredom and pay back the officers'. With curly hair and a goatee beard that hinted at an adventurous spirit, he merged well the sailors.

At sea on Saturday and Sunday nights, there was an issue of brandy and port to the ship's company — enough for a round of toasts. There was the sailors' toast 'To Sweethearts and Wives', another to 'The Old Folks at Home', and for good measure there was the universal 'Slainte Mhath' — 'Good Health' in Gaelic.[13] For the rest of the week the liquor was kept under lock and key in the ship's bond store and, as Murray wrote ruefully, 'presided over by the mate [chief officer] like an ogre'. Murray preferred the brandy on board to the whisky, and helped himself to a bottle of it one day when he came across the key in the door of the store.

After riding the roaring forties all the way from Cape Town, past The Snares and up the east coast of the South Island of New Zealand, *Nimrod* reached Lyttelton on 23 November, three and a half months after setting out from Torquay. Expedition manager Alfred Reid was already in Christchurch, drumming up publicity in advance of Shackleton's arrival from Australia in the second week of December, ordering fresh produce for *Nimrod*'s voyage to the Ice, and checking out the newly arrived Manchurian ponies on an island in Lyttelton Harbour. According to their New Zealand trainer, they were 'very wild' on arrival. The *Lyttelton Times* preview coverage of the expedition was spread across nine columns.

Disembarking at Melbourne, Shackleton wasted no time winning public support, and the government's as well. He presented public lectures in Melbourne and Sydney that were prearranged by an eminent geology professor, T. W. Edgeworth David, of the University of Sydney, who had a special interest in the processes of glaciation but little opportunity to observe them in Australia. Melbourne responded enthusiastically, but Sydney was even more caught up in the spirit of Antarctic discovery. Over 4000 people turned up to Shackleton's Sydney lecture, described by David in a telegram to Mrs Shackleton as 'brilliant'. The Australian government thought likewise, announcing a £5,000 contribution towards the expedition. Instead of banking the public donations arising from the two lectures, Shackleton passed them on to local charities, a gesture that further endeared him to the Australian people and institutions.

Professor David, a slightly built but agile Welshman in his late forties who had worked in earth sciences in Australia for 25 years, had a stake in talking up the importance of Antarctic research to the nation, having been invited by Shackleton earlier in the year to join the expedition as far as King Edward VII Land.[14] The Australian government's grant encouraged Shackleton to expand his team. On David's advice, he engaged Douglas Mawson, an ambitious and energetic lecturer in mineralogy and petrology at Adelaide University, aged 25. David was his teacher and mentor. Mawson's title with the expedition was 'Physicist', although his field was geology. Mad keen on a polar adventure, he was not in the mood to argue the toss over his designation and, anyway, Shackleton probably had magnetism, a branch of physics, in mind when he labelled Mawson's role. A third Australian earth scientist, Leo

Cotton, was also invited to sail with *Nimrod* to Antarctica and back.

From Shackleton's Australian visit there was one more addition to the shore party: Australian-born Bertram Armytage. In fact, he was the only member of the party not born in the British Isles and Ireland. Shackleton needed someone familiar with horses to look after the Manchurian ponies with Mackay and be available for general duties. At 38, Armytage had had various jobs, including service in the South African War.

On 13 December, Shackleton landed in New Zealand, caught up with his manager and was thrown immediately into a hectic schedule of public lectures at Wellington and Christchurch; social lunches, parties and media interviews; a number of meetings with Christchurch businessman Joseph Kinsey, an English-born shipping company principal who had been appointed the expedition's New Zealand agent;[15] and calls on the prime minister and other dignitaries.

The New Zealand government, noting the grant by the Australian government, pondered what it should contribute to the expedition coffers and decided £1,000 was an appropriate amount. The Shackleton lectures, as inspirational as those in Australia, garnered donations amounting to several hundred pounds at each venue. These funds were straight away handed over to New Zealand charitable causes, a gesture that left the New Zealand public thinking Shackleton was a saint and the British Antarctic Expedition of 1907 was okay financially.

On the eve of *Nimrod*'s departure for the Ice, Shackleton wrote a long letter to his wife. It contained phrase after effusive phrase of loving, caring thoughts for her and their two children, and some words about the challenge ahead: ' . . . we will do our best to win . . . ours is a big work and if we carry through it will be worth it . . .'

'For a joint scientific and geographical piece of organization give me Scott; for a Winter Journey, Wilson; for a dash to the Pole and nothing else, Amundsen; and if I am in a devil of a hole and want to get out of it, give me Shackleton every time.'

— Apsley Cherry-Garrard,
The Worst Journey in the World, 1922

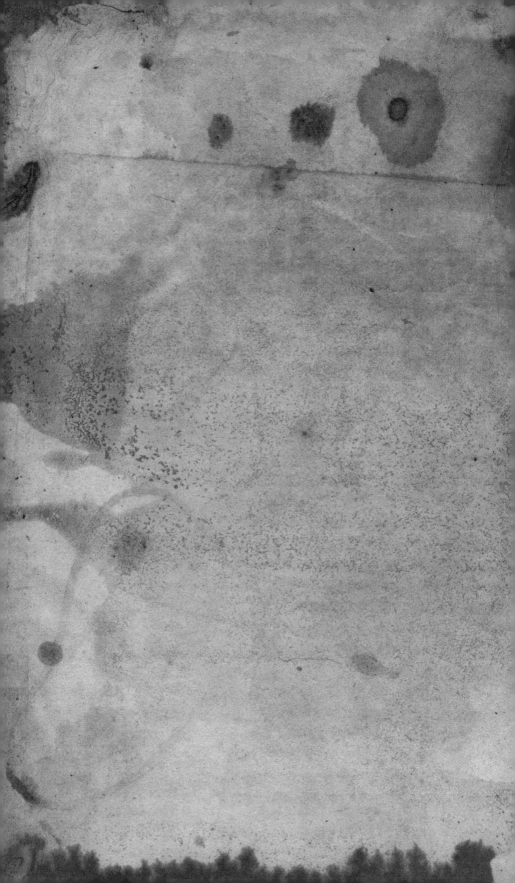

PART
2
THE
Expedition

9 —
A WILD RIDE TO
THE PACK ICE

New Year's Day 1908 was Regatta Day on Lyttelton Harbour. The crowds, flags and saluting guns, together with a cacophony of ships' sirens, made it seem as if royalty had turned up for the event at Christchurch's proud port town of Lyttelton, perched beside the harbour nestling in an extinct, eroded volcano. But no, the centre of attention on 1 January 1908 was simply a converted old sealing vessel on her way to Antarctica and so heavily laden that her Plimsoll (load) line was submerged. The Union Steam Ship Company steamer *Koonya* was assigned to take her in tow as far as the pack ice. Coal was crucial for the year-long expedition, and the tow would conserve it.

There were thousands of well-wishers on the docks and hillside vantage points that afternoon — more than 30,000 — and several thousand more on the water aboard a flotilla of launches, excursion vessels and liners, some of which listed dangerously as passengers mobbed on one side or the other for a view. Brass bands marched to stirring music through the main street. Cargo ships in port blasted the summer air with their horns, and from the crews of three British warships *Nimrod* received a thunderous three cheers. The cruiser HMS *Powerful*, flagship of the Royal Navy's Sydney-based squadron and three and a half times *Nimrod*'s length, flew ceremonial pennants fore and aft, dwarfing the expedition ship. Gun emplacements overlooking the harbour entrance, a legacy of the 'Russian Scare' some 20 years earlier, boomed their own salutes.

No one could recall a ship's farewell that was as noisy and fervent as this one — it topped even the enthusiastic send-off for Scott's Discovery expedition seven years earlier. *Nimrod*'s modest size did not matter. *Discovery* was 12 metres longer and much more beamy, her internal spaces more than doubling the gross tonnage of *Nimrod*. What did matter was the Shackleton factor: his winning personality coupled with his captivating goal — to reach the end of the Earth, the South Pole. Could a private venture like his go where no one had gone before? The people of Christchurch were fascinated.

The immense crowd farewelling *Nimrod* could see she meant business. She sat deeply in the water, overloaded and underpowered, with her freeboard measuring little more than a metre — not a lot to spare in the face of the world's stormiest ocean.

Down aft and below the main deck lay the whisky and other liquor, locked up in the bond store. Of the estimated 228 tonnes of cargo on board, including 10 ponies (there was not enough room for all 15, the number originally intended to be taken) and 10 tonnes of pony fodder, the liquor made up a tonne or thereabouts, roughly half of it whisky. Two barrels of beer from J. Speight and Co., the celebrated Dunedin brewery, were winched aboard at Lyttelton. Also loaded here were two kinds of liqueur — crème de menthe and orange curaçao. No one in the shore party — least of all Frank Wild, who was in charge of the provisions and no doubt had a say in their make-up — could complain about a limited choice in alcohol for the special occasion or nightcap. Whisky, brandy, port, champagne, wine, liqueurs, cider and beer were stowed in *Nimrod*, and for a non-alcoholic pick-me-up or sustenance beverage the expedition also had a choice — teas of various kinds, hot milk, cocoa, coffee, lime juice. The stocks of cocoa alone weighed almost half a tonne.

Shackleton knew from his experience with the Discovery expedition, as well as from Scott's own reports, that New Zealand could supply quality food and other provisions at a reasonable price, and that there was a fair chance of some items being donated. Above all, New Zealand offered 'fresh' foodstuffs — meat, vegetables and fruit. The fact that Lyttelton was the leaping-off place for the Ross Sea region of Antarctica meant that the fresh or chilled supplies loaded at Lyttelton would be preserved in the hold within a few days of departure when the ship would enter the subantarctic zone. At the time, Shackleton considered fresh meat as useful as fresh fruit and vegetables for combating scurvy, the bugbear of long-distance mariners and polar explorers on marathon sledge journeys.

Donated by Canterbury farmers and stock firms, 32 sheep were taken aboard the *Koonya* alive and kicking, for transfer to *Nimrod* at the end of the tow as carcasses. More than two tonnes of canned beef, mutton and chops, sheep's tongues and sausages were supplied by Christchurch and Wellington meat companies. New Zealand dairy products — milk powder, butter and cheese — were loaded, along with 120 dozen eggs packed in salt for longevity. Nine huskies, progeny of sled dogs left at Stewart Island by a Norwegian-led Antarctic expedition in 1900, were housed on deck.[16]

The Boss: Ernest Shackleton at Cape Royds
in an authoritative pose.
THE HEART OF THE ANTARCTIC

The Nimrod Hut during the winter of 1908.
THE HEART OF THE ANTARCTIC

The Nimrod Hut with packing cases piled against its weather wall and ice blocks dangling from the eaves, part of an evaporation experiment.
THE HEART OF THE ANTARCTIC

Steam rises from a canvas bath in the Nimrod Hut.
The bather is said to be Alistair Mackay.
THE HEART OF THE ANTARCTIC

This corner cubicle, occupied by David and Mawson, was known as 'The Pawn Shop'. The door opens into the darkroom.
SCOTT POLAR RESEARCH INSTITUTE, REF P98/9/16

Gramophone music was popular in the winter evenings and at times of celebration. George Marston is operating it.
CANTERBURY MUSEUM, REF. 1981.110.36

The New Zealand government, besides chipping in £1,000 in cash for the expedition, covered half the cost of the *Koonya's* tow, with the Union Steam Ship Company donating the other half. New Zealand premier Sir Joseph Ward presented Shackleton with New Zealand postage stamps in a brass cylinder for placing at the South Pole, should the expedition reach it, and the New Zealand postmaster general officially appointed Shackleton as Antarctic postmaster to handle shore-party mail returning with *Nimrod*.[17]

Across New Zealand and Australia public interest was colossal. Antarctica was extraterrestrial, the nearest thing to exploring another planet. In New Zealand Shackleton had received more than 500 applications from expedition hopefuls. But *Nimrod* was full to overflowing. Among the last to join the ship's company was a well-off Mid-Canterbury farmer and master mariner, George Buckley, who had 'impetuously' asked if he could travel as far as the pack ice. Shackleton 'impulsively' agreed, aware of Buckley's sea experience and, more important, his donation of £500 towards the expedition. With minutes to spare and only an overnight bag for luggage, the New Zealander scrambled aboard dressed in a summer suit. The last member of the shore party to board was the slim and nimble Professor David, who had spent the hour before cast-off rounding up the geological equipment still on shore, including ice-coring gear and all manner of glassware and other apparatus. It had almost been overlooked. Gingerly carrying the last armful of delicate equipment up the gangway and looking a bit like the proverbial absent-minded professor, David was confronted by a woman of ample girth scurrying off, scared she might soon find herself bound for Antarctica. Whereupon the professor was toppled off the gangway — 'charged down by superior weight' was how Shackleton described the incident — but fortunately landed among

Nimrod leaving Lyttelton under tow by the Union Steam Ship Company freighter *Koonya*.
CANTERBURY MUSEUM, REF 1940.193.201

some of the expedition members. There was no injury or damage to David and his gear, allowing *Nimrod* to slip away from the crowded wharves at the appointed hour of 4 p.m.

Out near the harbour entrance, after passing the visiting British warships, *Nimrod* picked up the hawser from *Koonya*. Made from steel wire, and measuring 10 centimetres thick and 220 metres long, it was fastened to two weighty chain cables extending from either side of the expedition vessel's bow — shock-absorbers to mitigate jerking by the larger towing vessel. Then *Nimrod's* engines fell silent. What no one seemed to have predicted was that the bow would be weighed down by seven tonnes of chain, making *Nimrod* susceptible to waves washing across her decks in heavy weather from a southerly quarter.

Heavy weather was not long in arriving. Any expectation there would be evening drinks to celebrate departure for the Ice was dashed for some expedition members by seasickness and for others by living spaces less salutary than those on offer at the United Service Hotel or Warners in central Christchurch or aboard the UK–Australia liner *Runic*. Gone were the *Runic's* spacious, well-appointed lounges, fine dining, seductive bars and evening entertainment. *Nimrod* was a shock.

Soon almost everyone on board was seasick, even seasoned sailors, some of whom had never experienced seas as rough as this. Expedition doctor Eric Marshall was 'sick as hell'. For the first few nights he eschewed the shore party's allocated bunkroom aft, 'Oyster Alley', preferring the wardroom floor or the warm engine room.

Oyster Alley — the Scientists' Quarters — was even more of a challenge for its occupants, whose numbers had increased from a pair (Murray and Mackay on the voyage to New Zealand) to a dozen. Luggage and scientific gear were crammed into a bunk-lined cabin measuring 5 metres by 2.5 metres, with just one small ventilator. Oyster Alley was, to put it mildly, a dimly lit squeeze. 'An awful hole' is how geologist Douglas Mawson described it. Entry to it was by a manhole and ladder. For the next four and a half weeks this would be their accommodation. Young Raymond Priestley described it as 'more like my idea of Hell than anything I have ever imagined'. Marshall described the air as foul — 'one wakes up gasping for breath' — and Brocklehurst labelled it 'poisonous'. Shackleton, meanwhile, and the second-oldest member of his shore party, James Murray, shared the cabin of *Nimrod*'s master, Captain Rupert England, a 29-year-old Yorkshireman.

The main space for socialising and for dining was the ship's wardroom, an impossibly small area for the expedition team and officers, 23 all told.

In the stormy conditions, which prevailed for much of the first week, the crowded aft cabin was exceedingly damp. Wrote Mawson: 'We are wet all day by waves and sleep in wet clothes between wet blankets at night.' Water sloshed about the floor. On one especially rough day, seas washing across the main deck and penetrating below threatened to extinguish the boiler fires. Abject misery was the lot of those prone to motion sickness: 'I noticed a geologist washing about in the scuppers,' observed James Murray during one very rough day, 'quite indifferent whether he went overboard or stayed on the ship.' This was probably Mawson, who suffered severe motion sickness. On a day when the seas were mountainous Marshall was caught on the main deck when one wave came on board, swamping him up to his waist. Only a lifeline on deck saved him. He wore the same clothes, wet through, for 10 days.

The latitudes of the roaring forties turned into the furious fifties and gales from the south and west created valleys in the dark water so deep that at times little *Nimrod* all but disappeared from the towing vessel's view. The pitching (up to 45 degrees) and rolling (as much as 55 degrees) took its toll. One pony, badly injured, had to be shot; a sled dog died of exposure.

The constant turmoil on board and the need to keep at least one hand free to move safely about the vessel meant there were few occasions for a pleasant drink. The liquor itself must have been securely stowed aft. No reports emerged of storm damage in the bond store — shattered cases or broken bottles.

On 14 January, in a smoother seaway, *Koonya* and *Nimrod* encountered ice floes and tabular icebergs with blue-green caves in them. They had reached the pack ice, close to the Antarctic Circle, where there is round-the-clock daylight in the southern summer. Time for the tow to end. They had come 1490 nautical miles (2760 km) from Lyttelton, two-thirds of the distance to the Great Ice Barrier.

Before the vessels parted, though, there was an exchange — the affable Ashburton farmer George Buckley went one way by bucking whaleboat, sheep the other by line. *Koonya* briefly became a meatworks as the sheep on board her were slaughtered to provide fresh meat for the expedition. Ten carcasses attached to a buoyed line were successfully transferred to *Nimrod,* but then the line parted and a second lot ended up as 'food for the albatrosses'. Buckley, admired for his willingness to man the pumps and look after the ponies and dogs, received a champagne toast from his *Nimrod* shipmates before departing for New Zealand with *Koonya.*

Buckley's popularity, his willingness to pitch in and his way with the animals may have caused Shackleton to contemplate

Only the masts and funnel of *Koonya* are visible from *Nimrod* as a monster wave is about to break over the expedition ship. It caused considerable damage.
THE HEART OF THE ANTARCTIC

adding him to the shore party. But his team was large enough already. The cramped, uncomfortable and wave-tossed entrée to Antarctica had been a real test of character, and Shackleton — the Boss, as he would commonly be called from now on — had used the voyage south to assess 'bodily or temperamental weakness' among his men.

The next challenge was to set up camp.

10 —
THE BARRIER

Eight days after *Koonya* dropped the tow and turned back, Shackleton is on the bridge of *Nimrod* gazing at a gigantic wall of ice, the Great Ice Barrier, an electrifying vista for any polar explorer. Ahead of the ship is nothing but sea and sky divided by the band of ice. Shackleton's first reaction is one of awe — that nature could construct such a thing. Cliffs of ice extending as far as the eye can see in either direction. Cliffs pocked by caverns, but elsewhere presenting sides as smooth and tough as worked steel. As *Nimrod* edges closer, the scale of the cliffs hits home — for the most part, they are much taller than the masts. Gone are the mountainous seas of the circumpolar Southern Ocean, unimpeded by land or ice. Here the sea is tamer. Ice commands this region.

Shackleton is dressed in a thick woollen polo-neck jumper, with whiskers thickening to combat the cold. Switching from his explorer's sense of wonder to the practical realities, he adopts a typical pose, fists on hips, his broad brow creased in concentration. There is a decision to be made that will define the course of this expedition. One scenario is to set up camp on the Barrier ice edge as a launch pad for the South Pole, the closest

Nimrod in pack ice.
CANTERBURY MUSEUM,
REF 19XX.2.604

approach a ship can make to it. No previous expedition has dared establish a base on the ice shelf. Shackleton knows that if he could do so, the Pole would be closer than if it were approached from the southern end of Ross Island — about 140 kilometres less sledging. A psychological boost at the very least.

He was here six years earlier as a junior officer with the Discovery expedition. *Nimrod* is close now to the piece of ice shelf where Scott's expedition inflated a large hydrogen balloon with a basket underslung to take the first aerial photographs of Antarctica. A low stretch of cliffs made access relatively easy then. No one knew the inland extent of the Barrier, later renamed the Ross Ice Shelf.[18] Fed by glaciers flowing from Antarctica's elevated ice cap, it is the world's largest ice shelf, the size of Texas. Filling the inner half of the Ross Sea, it is moving north at glacial speed. Except that the ice shelf, generally 50 to 350 metres thick, is afloat. And its front is an iceberg factory, calving continuously.

Which is why Shackleton is struggling now to recognise the Barrier edge, in particular the bight where Borchgrevink landed and a nearby bay that Scott named Balloon Inlet. Nowhere are the cliffs low enough for a ship to safely come alongside.

There is discussion between Shackleton, the expedition leader, and Captain England, the master of the vessel, whose main concern is her safety and, in theory, whose say is final. Factors for debate include the dwindling coal supply and the prospect of sea ice re-forming in another month or so. There is little time to spare. England is four years younger than Shackleton, on his first Antarctic voyage as skipper, and nervous.

As *Nimrod* steams along the southernmost reach of the Barrier's cliff edge Shackleton tries to make sense of its different profile and changed alignment. He concludes that Borchgrevink's

Bight and Balloon Inlet have disappeared through a colossal calving that has wiped out the two features and created a huge notch, 15 kilometres wide, in the edge of the Barrier. Perhaps this is the source of the sprawling herd of tabular icebergs encountered a few days earlier near the pack ice. Shackleton soon has a name for the Barrier's new bay. Several hundred whales, humpbacks or right whales, appear on the seaward side of the ship, cavorting at the height of the breeding season. There are spouts and raised tail flukes everywhere. The Bay of Whales it is, the world's most southerly stretch of open sea.[19]

But a name is not a foothold. Everyone on board is anxious for a decision on where to erect the expedition's hut. The Bay of Whales is ruled out — towards the head of the bay there is far too much sea ice for *Nimrod* to penetrate. This news delights the geologists, who would have had to sledge about 120 kilometres to locate the nearest rocks.

Now *Nimrod* continues on an eastward track for King Edward VII Land, the Barrier's eastern buttress. This and McMurdo Sound, the *Discovery*'s old base, are the only possibilities. England favours McMurdo; Eric Marshall, the shore party's burly surgeon, accuses Shackleton of a lack of courage ('hasn't got the guts of a louse') if he does not try for King Edward VII Land; and Shackleton worries about breaking his promise to Scott about avoiding McMurdo Sound. Even at this distance from England, polar politics puts more bite into the freezing air.

After another day's sailing eastward and still a good distance from land, *Nimrod* is thwarted by dense pack ice, snow squalls and fog, and turns for McMurdo, tracking back along the edge of the Barrier. It is 25 January. The short Antarctic summer is well advanced. The captain is deeply worried about having enough fuel to get back to New Zealand, and Shackleton tells him to conserve coal by burning the 'easily available woodwork' on the ship, even sections of mast if necessary.

On 28 January they catch their first glimpse of Mount Erebus, Ross Island's massive volcano,[20] and spirits lift with a 'Splice the Mainbrace' party in the evening — drinks and music in honour of Prof David's 50th birthday. Even Raymond Priestley, who generally refrains from alcohol, is moved to drink the professor's health. For David, dubbed 'a grand old chap' by one of the ship's officers, it is a double celebration. Instead of returning home to resume teaching at the end of the long university vacation, he will be joining the shore party, at Shackleton's invitation, as head of the scientific staff.

With Erebus on the horizon, excitement on board begins to build. This is what Shackleton lives for: challenges in pristine, unexplored places at the end of the Earth, where man meets untrammelled nature on nature's terms and adventure that borders on the mystical. But when great stress and danger appear, as must inevitably happen in such an extreme environment, a lesser person could be driven to drink.

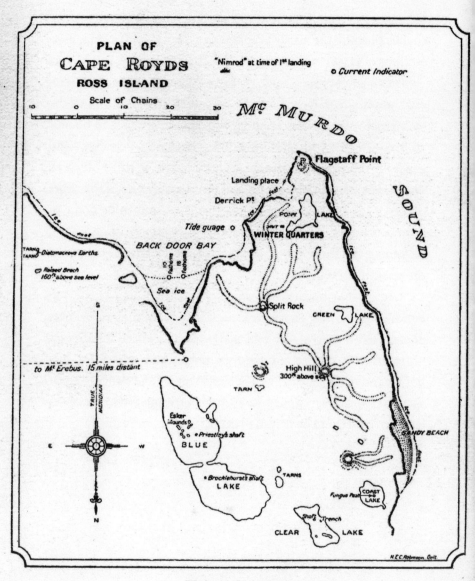

WINTER QUARTERS

THE HEART OF THE ANTARCTIC

BRITISH ANTARCTIC
EXPEDITION 1907

170S

Loading venesta cases at
Lyttelton, December 1907.
ROYAL GEOGRAPHICAL SOCIETY,
REF S00161130

11 —
LANDING
AT ROYDS

The first serious imbibing of strong drink on the expedition — at least the first to be reported — occurred soon after the ponies were offloaded from *Nimrod*. The ship had arrived at McMurdo Sound on 31 January. She was greeted by a continuous expanse of sea ice two metres thick that halted her progress south, 20 kilometres from Scott's old base at Hut Point. Over the next couple of days, three members of the shore party — Adams, Wild and Joyce — walked to Hut Point over the sea ice, looking for cracks. They returned having found none, therefore no possibility of *Nimrod*'s reaching the Discovery Hut. Towards midnight on 3 February, with very little choice in the matter of where to base the expedition, Shackleton went over to Cape Royds, a promontory of black volcanic rock and nesting Adelie penguins while *Nimrod* drifted to and fro in the breezes.[21] Shackleton landed there with Captain England and Chief Engineer Harry Dunlop. Walking past groups of nesting penguins, they came to an iced-over lake and above it a flattish area in a hollow that Shackleton reckoned would be 'an ideal spot' for their winter quarters. The site had a north-facing aspect and a magnificent outlook, and it offered some shelter from the prevailing southeast winds.

Now the unloading could begin — 'the most uncomfortable fortnight, and hardest work, full of checks and worries, that I or any other member of the party had ever experienced,' wrote Shackleton. They worked around the clock, virtually non-stop and sometimes for more than 24 hours at a stretch, with the ship pulling alongside the shifting, cracking sea ice and hardly ever coming closer than 300 metres to the headland.

The Arrol-Johnston motor car was the first big item winched off the ship, followed by the eight surviving ponies (a second pony had been shot on the voyage south after becoming ill and covered in sores). The ponies were deposited on the sea ice in a horsebox and led ashore by way of a network of floes and fast ice. Soon they were harnessed up to haul stores stacked on sledges over the sea ice between the ship and the landing place. Alistair Mackay, assistant surgeon, was leading one of the ponies, called Chinaman, across a six-inch crack in the sea ice when the horse took fright, reared up and backed off the floe — straight into the freezing sea.

Mackay kept a firm grip on Chinaman's head rope and with the help of others encouraged him to scramble his forelegs onto the floe. From there, with ropes slung around his body, he was pulled to safety. Safety? Having spent several minutes immersed in water below freezing point, he trembled all over, at risk of hypothermia. Would something medicinal help? Whisky, perhaps? Or brandy? Someone brought a full bottle of brandy from the ship and, according to Shackleton, half of it was poured down Chinaman's throat. Another diary account of the incident, written by a Scottish crew member, fireman Felix Rooney, suggests that Chinaman swallowed most of the bottle 'and it is believed that this saved

Landing stores after ice broke away from the edge of the headland.
THE HEART OF THE ANTARCTIC

his life'. (Rooney allegedly reported that the man who poured the brandy down the pony's throat afterwards poured some down his own.) *Nimrod* was pressed into action as a result of the incident, pushing the wayward floe back against the fast ice to tighten the sea ice and secure a route to shore for the ponies.

Next came the ordeal of conveying the stores and equipment to Cape Royds, including the liquor. With the sea ice continually swinging and cracking, *Nimrod* was hardly ever in the same place. One day she could be as close as 300 metres to Flagstaff Point and several icy or cliffed landing places; the next she might be lying well over a kilometre away. The venesta cases, 2500 of them, were transported by sledge or rowboat, depending on the access. Ice around the headland was in the process of breaking up during the transfer of cargo ashore, forcing the cargo handlers to use *Nimrod*'s whaleboat for much of the time. 'O for a motor boat or even an outboard motor, but we have none of these luxuries,' wrote fireman Rooney.

Frequently there were interruptions while *Nimrod* herself had to be manoeuvred. Ponies pulled sledges, men loaded and unloaded, winched and carried, and hauled on ropes. There were strained backs.

A horrible injury happened early on, when provisions were being retrieved from *Nimrod*'s after hatch. A crate hook manoeuvring one of the beer casks loaded in New Zealand swung free across the deck and struck the ship's second officer, Aeneas Mackintosh, in the right eye. His eye was badly mauled — the lens detached and a part of the retina was protruding — and Dr Marshall was forced to remove the eye in an operation conducted on the floor of the captain's cabin with Mackintosh under chloroform (also atropine and cocaine) and the surgeon kneeling.

Lifting stores up the cliff at Derrick Point, with *Nimrod* standing well off Cape Royds.
THE HEART OF THE ANTARCTIC

Pony Quan hauling sledges
with stores, January 1908.
THE HEART OF THE ANTARCTIC

For Mackintosh, the pain of the injury and operation was as nothing compared to the distress of the decision to send him back to New Zealand with *Nimrod*. He had been added to the shore party by Shackleton and was eagerly anticipating a year at Cape Royds.

Meanwhile, stress levels increased as time went on. *Nimrod's* management came under fire from members of the shore party, who considered Captain England cautious to the point of incompetent. He had kept *Nimrod* too far out. Shackleton had arguments with him, too, especially over the sharing of coal between the shore party for the year ahead and the ship for her return voyage. But he did warn his expedition team to guard against insubordination. They could be sent home for such transgressions. This tense time between the leader and his team was a singular low point in the entire expedition.

Towards the end of the unloading, with the sea ice retreating, coal had to be rowed a long way ashore before being lugged up the cliff in sacks with block-and-tackle and a derrick boom.

There were three coal dumps on the cape. Other cargo was stacked haphazardly, reflecting the scramble to get the necessities of life ashore.

Fatigue set in.

Shackleton, in his 1909 book of the expedition, *The Heart of the Antarctic*, described the scene he came upon one morning on board *Nimrod*.

> The men were certainly worn out. Davis' head [First
> Officer John Davis] had dropped on the wardroom
> table, and he had gone sound asleep with his spoon
> in his mouth, to which he had conveyed some of his

breakfast. Cotton [Australian geologist Leo Cotton,
supernumerary] had fallen asleep on the platform
of the engine-room steps, whilst Mawson, whose
lair was a little store-room in the engine-room,
was asleep on the floor. His long legs, protruding
through the doorway, had found a resting place
on the crosshead of the engine, and his dreams
were mingled with a curious rhythmical motion
which was fully accounted for when he woke up, for
the ship having got under way, the up-and-down
motion of the piston had moved his limbs with every
stroke. The sailors also were fast asleep . . .

Shackleton decided work would resume at 1 p.m., and he told England that when the coal supply on board had reduced to 93 tonnes, *Nimrod* could sail north — at the latest, the end of February.

The site for the hut had been decided at the outset, but construction of the building took 10 days, starting with the foundations. They needed to be rock-solid to withstand the blizzard gales. Chief Engineer Dunlop was in charge of the project. He ordered 22 post holes dug in the frozen ground with chisel, hammer and drill. A frozen slurry of the sandy volcanic soil and water locked the posts into place.

There were constant distractions with the unloading of supplies, and long waits sometimes for those waiting at the edge of the fast ice or on the rocky outcrop at Derrick Point, where coal and other supplies were hoisted up a low cliff. Not long after the dogs had been brought over, including six pups born on the voyage, an awful racket was heard coming from the adjacent penguin colony. Several huskies had escaped their leads and were running amok among the penguins. By the time the mayhem ended, 100 Adelies in a population of close to 4000 were dead and mobs of skuas were scavenging more frantically than usual.

The hut builders worked with a passion, putting the expedition's home together according to the Knightsbridge kitset-maker's instructions. The building gang and the shore cargo handlers were fed from a cookhouse fashioned out of a canvas cover propped up by oars. Later, bales of fodder were commandeered for a more roomy cookhouse before the hut was ready for occupying. As for sleeping arrangements, you slept in the open where you could and, in the absence of darkness, at any hour.

By 10 February the framework for the hut was up. To facilitate construction the fir weatherboards had been marked, morticed and tenoned in London, and iron cleats and tie rods reinforced roof and walls. The roof itself, mounted over trusses of Scots pine, was the epitome of secure design — two layers of canvas or heavy roofing felt sandwiching a 25 millimetre-thick layer of tongue-and-groove boards, with the whole roof criss-crossed by timber battens and held down by a pair of 17.5 millimetre-thick wire ropes anchored to timber deadmen in the frozen ground.

On 15 February, in honour of Shackleton's 34th birthday, there was a party on board *Nimrod*, an occasion that warranted tapping the first of the barrels of beer brought south. According to Philip Brocklehurst, Alistair Mackay was the 'most gay' of those who sampled the beer. Up late, Mackay, as a prank, 'put a live penguin in with Wild and Marston' and insisted on going to bed with his boots on.

A few days later the hut was closed in, and the stately Smith & Wellstood (Mrs Sam) coal stove was operational — a symbol of sustenance and warmth in a frozen desert setting. Not before time, either. Two days later Cape Royds was swallowed up by a blizzard.

From 20 to 22 February the blizzard hammered the headland and McMurdo Sound. Ferocious southeast gusts from the direction of Back Door Bay came whipping over the low ridge and shook the hut. The two windows on the south side were boarded up, and stayed that way for the rest of the year as a precaution against recurring storms. On the opposite, more sheltered side, stables for the eight ponies were fashioned from cases of maize, bales of fodder and a canvas tarpaulin. Dog kennels were also arrayed along the lee side of the hut.

Sea spray from the open water mixed with the blowing snow to coat the clusters of stores scattered about the volcanic rock and scoria environs. As temperatures plummeted from minus eight degrees Celsius to a shocking minus 27, successive coatings of water and snow turned to ice. Offshore, *Nimrod* took the full force of the storm. Despite lying bow on to the 160 km/h winds and breaking waves with her engines at 'full ahead', she was blown out of the sound, way beyond the northern end of Ross Island. Crew members wielding axes had to chip constantly at ice as it collected on her wooden surfaces. The rudder threatened to freeze up.

Shackleton and several others from the shore party who happened to be aboard *Nimrod* when the blizzard struck could do nothing but sit out the storm at sea. When they finally got ashore, they were impressed at how well the hut had stood up to what was called a 'tempest'. Stores depots, equipment stacks and coal dumps were deeply buried under ice. The men ashore figured that encasement in ice was all that saved their precious provisions from being blown to hell and gone.

Those who weathered the storm at the hut complained of how cold the interior was, even with the coal range roaring. The tongue-in-groove spruce floorboards were at or below freezing point. Shackleton directed that a wall of venesta cases be stacked against the vertical weatherboards on the south and east sides of the hut, almost to the height of the eaves, to help insulate the walls against wind chill. Six hundred cases were used in this way. Volcanic sand was poured into the gaps between the boxes to improve the insulation. The wall of cases also created an airlock in the crawl space under the floor. This space, accessed from near the entrance, was 1.2 metres deep at the front of the hut and narrowed down to meet the scoria at the inland end. It was the kind of space where supplies not immediately needed could be stowed. Cases of whisky and brandy were among the backup provisions placed here, where their very low freezing point spared them from damage by the elements.

On either side of the porch were small 'rooms'. To the right, closed in by biscuit cases, felt and canvas was Frank Wild's food store — he was in charge of issuing all foodstuffs; on the left was Mawson's chemical and physical laboratory. Only nominally a lab, it lacked a floor and was seldom warmer than the surrounding air. For the duration, it would find use mainly as a cold store. It was appropriately decorated with dangling ice crystals that grew from a stream of warm, moist air emerging from inside the hut when the inner porch door was opened.

The expedition's latrine was a makeshift 'dunny' built of timber and canvas on the lee side of the hut next to the lab, and behind it was the garage for the motor car, which was destined to be more a frustrating plaything than a valued workhorse. It struggled pitifully in snow and found use only on the hard, temporary sea ice.

As the winds died down on 22 February, *Nimrod*'s crew and the shore party set to work again unloading the last of the stores: packing cases, most of which contained liquid items that would require storage inside the hut, scientific equipment and more coal. They worked a long day, marvelling at how such a fierce storm could give way to a clear, soundless calm so suddenly.

By the evening Shackleton judged the coal supply ashore would be enough for their 12-month stay, although only just, and sent word to *Nimrod*'s captain to start out for New Zealand. England had his instructions, including a letter from Shackleton for the expedition's Christchurch agent, Joseph Kinsey, that would see him replaced as captain on the relief voyage by the *Koonya*'s captain, Frederick Evans.[22] England was ill, said Shackleton. He had lost his nerve for ice work.

At 10 p.m. *Nimrod* got under way to echoing cheers from ship and shore.

After the blizzard of February 1908, expedition members inspect snow and wind damage to the stores in front of the hut. The car is visible centre left.
CANTERBURY MUSEUM, REF 1981.10.2

12 —
CONVIVIAL IN
THEIR ISOLATION

After squalid Oyster Alley, stomach-churning seas, incessant damp, and the punishing experience of getting everything ashore and set up, the shore party could be forgiven for thinking they had taken over a picturesque holiday cottage with sea and mountain views. 'From the door of our hut, which faced northwest,' wrote the Boss, 'we commanded a splendid view of the sound and western mountains.' Picture Shackleton, an after-dinner cigarette in hand, at the outer door, watching the summer sun slip low over the Royal Society Range without setting. It cast pastel shades of green, gold and purple light across the sound and adjacent landscape — so much colour in an ostensibly black-and-white world. He had a foothold in Antarctica now — even if Scott asserted exclusive possession of this bit of it. Possession was said to be 'nine points of the law'. But occupation was a critical tenth! They were here and they were ready. Time for a toast to a successful landing?

Well, not yet — at least, not as far as diary records of the first day or two suggest. They were focused on settling in, with iced-up stores scattered like wayward knucklebones and more insulating to be done. Besides, domestic routines had yet to be worked out. The night of *Nimrod*'s departure was the first night the expedition's 15 men had been ashore together. They were the most isolated group of people in the world — exhausted and sleep-deprived to the point where isolation hardly registered with them.

Their first day as a shore party unsupported by ship was a Sunday, and Marshall in his diary expressed concern that there were no Sunday prayers, indeed no service at all since New Zealand. He also, and not for the first time, expressed misgivings about Shackleton. Although the two had managed to talk privately, they agreed to disagree on most occasions. Wrote Marshall: 'Shacks and I polite but distant, never will be any confidence between us.'

Typically, Antarctic expedition teams of the heroic age were a diverse lot (as they are in the modern era), and Shackleton's men were no different. They embodied expertise of many kinds, and personalities across the spectrum. Only three members of the team had previous experience of Antarctica. Shackleton, Wild and Joyce had been with Scott's Discovery expedition, although their accommodation had been the ship. This was their first experience of sharing a hut. What all now housed at Cape Royds had in common was an adventurous streak and an interest in exploring faraway lands. Having personally selected them, Shackleton knew he now had to build an esprit de corps. They had to work together; they were only as strong as their weakest link. The Boss signalled he would rely on everyone to play the role they were chosen to fill and that he would give each a free hand to pursue his specialist study or duty. At the same time, he intended to lead by example.

But first, there was some important housekeeping to attend to. Expedition members paired off and set up their bunks on either side of the main room, except for Shackleton, who acquired a relatively private space, his 'cabin', first turn right past the porch. It had a table in it and shelves for the expedition library and some of the surveying and scientific gear.

Each pair had a cubicle, barely two metres square, separated from the next one by sheets of canvas or sacking suspended from wires. Beds were built of the ever-present and versatile venesta cases or whatever else was available, including kerosene cases, spare lengths of timber and bamboo stakes. A mattress might comprise wood shavings covered with a blanket. Strips of canvas became stretchers. The cubicles reflected the individual taste and ingenuity of their inhabitants.

Cubicles also acquired nicknames. Adams, newly appointed second-in-command, and surgeon Marshall — the doctor may have fancied 2iC status himself — occupied the cubicle next door to Shackleton's cabin. It was dubbed 'No. 1 Park Lane'. Directly opposite was 'The Pawn Shop', where Prof David and Mawson lived in what they termed 'picturesque confusion' — a tangle of clothing, bedding, books and scientific gear. Their cubicle was also known as 'Old Curiosity Shop'. Opening off their cubicle was the expedition darkroom. Here, cases of wine were kept. Beside the two Australian geologists were the Discovery pair of Wild and Joyce, whose cubicle was proudly labelled 'The Rogues' Retreat'. It housed the printing press and was decorated by a Marston painting of two hardy blokes drinking beer from pint mugs. Further down the eastern side was the scientific pairing of Murray and Priestley, with Mackay and the cook, Roberts, occupying the corner. On the western side the last two cubicles housed Brocklehurst–Armytage ('Shruggery') and Marston–Day ('The Gables'). Marston had painted homely images on his cubicle's curtains, including a vase of flowers on a mantelpiece.

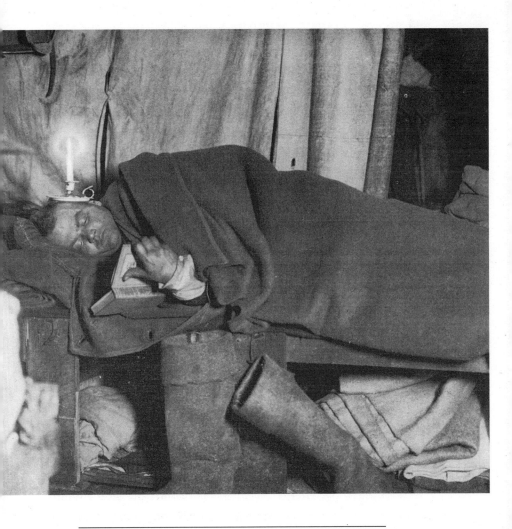

George 'Putty' Marston snuggled up with a book and a candle
balanced on his head.
SCOTT POLAR RESEARCH INSTITUTE, REF P68/76/108

At the far end were the stove, pantry-cum-bakery, cook's tables and storeroom. Squeezing into the middle of the hut between the two rows of cubicles was a trestle dining table nearly four metres long, which could be raised to the ceiling when not in use. It was another DIY product, built of packing cases with detachable legs.

For lighting there were two double-glazed windows on the northern wall and an array of gas lights, fuelled by a Drummond acetylene (carbide/water) gas generator suspended between Shackleton's cabin and the darkroom. Beneath it was a short corridor into the main room. A low beam supporting the generator spanned the corridor; a few heads were bumped on this beam, and it became a standing joke for the number of times it caught out all but the shortest members of the expedition — in fact, anyone over about 1.7 metres tall. Designed small, to maximise heat retention and economise on fuel, the hut was a cosy fit for 15 men, and at meal times it became a singularly convivial place.

From past experience, Shackleton knew three cooked meals a day would need to come off the Mrs Sam stove to sustain men working in a frozen environment. Roberts, a 35-year-old Englishman with a waggish sense of humour and an interest in zoology, was happy to oblige. He also produced loaves of bread and other baking daily.

Breakfast routinely began at 9 a.m., after the feeding of ponies and dogs and other chores. The men sat down at the dining table on bentwood chairs (to save weight on *Nimrod*, Shackleton had purchased very little furniture, expecting most to be fashioned from crates and other packaging). Bowls of steaming porridge were passed along the table from the stove end, and in turn the men helped themselves to sugar and hot milk from a large jug. Porridge was the breakfast staple dish, but there would be days when the cook offered a second course of bottled fruit — pears, apricots, plums, gooseberries and so on. 'Fruit days' were a treat. Breakfast tea was also served with milk made up from milk powder and heated. 'At twenty-five to ten breakfast was over,' said Shackleton, 'and then we had our smokes.' Cigarettes were popular, and the Boss smoked his fair share. Others preferred pipes. Inveterate pipe smokers made sure they were sucking on their pipe at photo opportunities. There were cigars as well for special occasions.

With enough food to last two years, Roberts could introduce plenty of variety and heartiness into the lunches and dinners. Meat from New Zealand, of which 'Koonya mutton' was the freshest, included roast beef, corned beef, Irish stew, ox cheeks, ox tongues and tripe in milk. Also in the larder for protein were York hams, bacon, brawn, salmon, sardines, pilchards and herrings. There were soups of many kinds, fresh vegetables from New Zealand and whole walls of canned vegies. Back in England, Colman's had donated a whopping six tonnes of flour — some 14,000 lb.

Cocoa was a popular drink during or after dinner. Shackleton was sure it had useful soporific properties that would come in handy. A good night's sleep was not always assured in a thinly walled dormitory whose 15 men were bound to include snorers.

In the week after *Nimrod* departed, the focus for everyone was on restoring order to the stores. With pick axes and crowbars, they attacked the ice imprisoning hundreds of cases that lay in jumbled piles. Another priority, a local harvest. On the other side of Pony Lake — a name applied to the ice-clad lake at their front door where the ponies were exercised — the Adelie penguin breeding season was fast drawing to a close. Many chicks had fledged, and the adults would soon be migrating north for the winter season. A few penguins were slaughtered to provide fresh meat in winter,

Adelie penguins nesting at
Cape Royds, 1908.
THE HEART OF THE ANTARCTIC

and seals were fair game as well. Seals were as much a resource for their blubber — used to fuel the stove — as for their rich meat. Both meat and blubber kept well without refrigeration.

It took some days and an increased effort at insulation before temperatures in the main room of the hut were anything like comfortable. Ink bottles inside the hut froze through those early days, shattering the glass. Prof David simply collected up the casts of solid ink, stowed them in a chilled place and melted them as required for writing his reports.

Outside, on a ridge immediately south of the hut, was a wooden structure housing meteorological equipment, and to the east, on another rise, Mawson set up an anemometer to record wind speeds. (Several times during the year it would measure winds exceeding 160 km/h or 100 miles an hour.)

Towards the end of February the sea ice broke out virtually all the way south to Hut Point. Even before *Nimrod* sailed there was water at least as far as the Erebus Ice Tongue, where the ship had offloaded supplies for the future use of southern sledging parties. Had *Nimrod* stayed two weeks longer she could well have landed the shore party at Hut Point. Ironically, the break-up of the sea ice increased the expedition's isolation. It closed the sea-ice 'road' south of Cape Royds until winter and spring refroze the sea.

But access south did not matter in the months leading up to winter, as there was plenty to do around the cape — more work than recreation.

Making the most of the warmest part of the year, biologist James Murray, often with the assistance of his amiable young roommate, Raymond Priestley, explored the local lakes for signs of life. There were five named lakes (Blue, Clear, Coast, Green and Pony) and numerous tarns within a kilometre of the hut. Blue Lake

George Marston and James
Murray relax at the door of the
Nimrod Hut on a sunny day.
THE HEART OF THE ANTARCTIC

was the largest, about 600 metres in length. Murray was delighted to find an abundance of things microscopic. They took the form of hardy aquatic creatures like rotifers, which are microscopic relatives of worms, and tardigrades, the tiny, charismatic 'water bears'. Cape Royds was the scenic lakes district of Ross Island. The geologists were also getting about and bending their knees, chipping away with hammers and collecting rock specimens from the volcanic slopes and outcrops of rare kenyte rock above the hut that were free of snow and ice. At little Coast Lake they cored the bottom strata and discovered to their surprise a thin layer of peat derived from fungi and moss. Did the whisky drinkers among the Nimrod shore party idly wonder whether it was good enough to infuse flavours into a Cape Royds home brew?

Ponies and dogs needed exercising and training. Bertram Armytage was in charge of the ponies, and Ernest Joyce was the dog handler, although others in the party were only too keen to help out. As Antarcticans of later decades were to discover, dog teams provided stimulation and distracted base staff from the psychological rigours of isolation. They kept folk sane. This was especially so in winter, when moonlit sledging was pretty well guaranteed to be an uplifting experience.

Then one pony, Zulu, went down writhing. Half a bottle of brandy was administered — a last resort, which had worked for Chinaman. It turned out to be a form of last rites. Zulu died of something corrosive in his stomach. More ponies succumbed; four altogether. Autopsies showed they had been eating the volcanic sand near the hut for its salt content (from salt spray deposited by the blizzard). The quantities proved fatal. It was an alarming development given that the South Pole Party would be relying largely on pony power to haul sledges. After the four deaths,

Armytage and the other handlers made sure the four survivors — Quan, Socks, Grisi and the sea-ice survivor Chinaman — were kept away from the sand. Curiously, the deceased ponies all had dark coats; the survivors had white coats or were lightly coloured. Shackleton remained confident the ponies would end up being more useful than the dogs: '. . . the pony is a far more efficient animal, one pony doing the work of at least ten dogs on the food allowance for ten dogs, and travelling a longer distance in a day'.

Hut routine required everyone to take a turn at messman and nightwatchman duties. There were no class or status divides here. Every two weeks your number would come up and, like it or not, no matter what your role you had to pitch in, the leader included. Shackleton would never ask any of his men to do tasks he was not prepared to tackle himself. He could turn his hand to managing a dog team, hauling a biologist's dredge line, test-driving the car, feeding the ponies or emptying the latrine bucket. Roster duties included keeping the stove stoked with coal or blubber, cleaning and tidying the hut's interior communal spaces, laying the table and washing up afterwards, collecting ice to melt on the coal range for the water supply, and generally assisting the cook, Roberts, who was awoken at 7.30 a.m. During the hours of sleep the nightwatchman might record the 'fitful phrases' of those who talked in their sleep and reprise them at the breakfast table. Lunch was served at 1 p.m., and dinner, the fullest meal of the day, at 6.30 sharp, after which tobacco would again be consumed in the form of pipes and cigarettes.

Outdoors during the daylight hours there was always something of interest going on — the retreat of the sea ice, Adelie and emperor penguins on the move, weather observations, lake and marine biology, and the world's southernmost active volcano right in your face every day, cloud permitting. Ross Island's high point, Mount Erebus, 3794 metres (12,448 feet), huffed and puffed most days, seemingly with a life force of its own — a monolith with a molten centre wrapped entirely in snow and ice. The lava lake at its summit was just 24 kilometres (15 miles) from the Nimrod expedition hut, and from it came clouds of steam and sometimes a plume of smoke tinged blue. It was a dynamic mountain backdrop. It had never been climbed.

Six weeks after *Nimrod*'s departure, plans were made for an ascent while there was still 24-hour daylight. For protection against the cold, the Nimrod expedition had brought with them a range of clothing, footwear, hats and gloves, most made of wool. The clothing included singlets, shirts, pants, mittens, scarves, caps, bedsocks and a pyjama suit of Jaeger wool. Other fibres included reindeer skin, wolfskin, dogskin and camel-hair. The soft-soled reindeer-skin boots, called finnesko, were lined with sedge grass, which improved insulation and kept feet as dry as possible. There were warm house-boots and Russian felt boots. Snow goggles came with red and green lenses. The tents were simple five-poled models made of light drill, a green colour 'restful to the eyes', with groundsheets. Including the poles and groundsheets, each tent pack weighed just 30 lb (13.6 kg).

Six men were selected — an ascent party and a support party. Geologists David and Mawson, accompanied by Mackay as medic, would climb to the summit; Adams, Marshall and Brocklehurst would provide support up to a certain altitude. Science and geographical exploration were twin goals, along with an opportunity to test gear and personnel, and practise camping and travel in snow and ice. On 5 March the climbers set off, hauling a sledge with food and equipment. After three days they were two-thirds the way up the mountain, then a blizzard kept them tent-bound for 32 hours.

With Brocklehurst laid up with frostbitten toes, the other five decided that rather than split up they would press on together to the summit and the rim of the active crater. Summiting in thin, subzero air through a belt of fumaroles, they took measurements and photographs, collected rock specimens, heard hissing and booming sounds, and watched volcanic mud flying and the mountain belching masses of steam. They did not dally. Altitude made breathing difficult. Going back down, they slithered, stumbled and glissaded their way off the main cone and down the lower slopes to arrive at Cape Royds the next day at 11 a.m., bruised from all the falling and 'dead tired' but elated by their achievement. They had been away six days.

At the hut they were greeted like conquering heroes. There were handshakes all round and corks popped off champagne bottles in what appears to have been the first celebratory drink at Cape Royds after Shackleton's birthday on 15 February. Shackleton noted that the bubbly 'tasted like nectar to the way-worn people'. Roberts produced, seemingly at a moment's notice, a sumptuous meal comprising hot porridge and milk, prime boiled ham, and fresh bread with lashings of fresh butter.

Prof David had shown that his age, 50, was not a barrier to high climbing. Nonetheless, he was overjoyed to be back at base: 'Delicious luxuriating in all the comforts of Antarctic civilization,' he wrote in his diary that night. 'Oh! the luxury of dry blankets after a stifling wet sleeping bag.'

The learned Welshman had established himself in the expedition team as a paragon of politeness and good manners, a kindly, avuncular figure with impressive stamina despite the grey hair.

Till now, personal diaries and journals were all but silent on the question of alcohol consumption. Notwithstanding the teetotal environment he grew up in, Shackleton tolerated drinking so long as it did not interfere with the work at hand or cause ructions. Moderation was now his message. He did not stand in the way of a hearty celebration with alcoholic drinks on appropriate occasions — or even the use of a few drinks to create a relaxed atmosphere — but he disdained drunkenness and especially anyone out of control because of drink. His preference was for a teetotal regime between celebrations. Parties should not go beyond a 'mild spree'.

As Frank Wild would recall years later in his memoirs, members of the expedition with a taste for alcohol could utilise their weekly allowance of 'one drink per man on a Saturday night'. There were toasts 'To Sweethearts and Wives', and wry comments about hoping they never met up.

Aware that booze and swearing were as allied as snow and ice, Shackleton also made known his objection to swearing to the point of cultivating an 'anti-swearing club'. Any club member caught swearing was fined one shilling.[23] Marshall, a non-smoker, promoted a comparable anti-smoking campaign — participants wanting to quit were charged £3 if caught lighting up a cigarette.

In the field some members of the expedition team are thought to have carried hip flasks of whisky and topped up the flasks back at base. Given the popular notion in Victorian and Edwardian society that whisky and brandy had restorative, medicinal or warming properties, no doubt some of the men brought this idea to the Ice. Beer, by contrast, might make you feel colder in a cold environment.

Frank Wild's interest in the barrels of beer shipped to Cape Royds prompted him one day to bring a barrel into the hut. It took three days to thaw. When tapped, it 'ran black'. About half a pint of this dark beer was served to those wishing to taste it. The effect, as Wild would report, was 'astonishing'. Seemingly, the freezing process had driven the colour and alcohol towards the centre of the barrel and after thawing, the concentrated contents were the first to be tapped. The following day the ration was described by Wild as 'very pale wishy washy stuff'.

On 19 March, artist George ('Putty') Marston, plump-cheeked and popular, with a prizefighter's build, turned 26 and there was a special dinner featuring turtle soup and roast blackcock, a kind of grouse, with rounds of cider and beer, and port to follow. This beer, too, was more potent than its New Zealand makers had intended, because the alcohol had been concentrated. It was quite a party, but probably within the bounds of what the Boss would accept — a 'mild spree'. There was a run of birthdays from March to May and most were celebrated with a special dinner, accompanied by beer, champagne and whisky. Whisky was introduced as a treat. The gramophone was always in use. Eric Marshall's birthday dinner featured treats such as turtle soup and tinned reindeer, plum pudding with brandy sauce, and crystallised fruits, accompanied throughout by champagne and whisky. For entertainment, Prof David read from Charles Dickens's first novel, *The Pickwick Papers*.

At Royds following the ascent of Erebus, Sir Philip Brocklehurst's frostbite remained a serious concern. As the youngest expedition member wrote, one of his feet looked 'a horrid sight, all black, red and green & all blown up'. He hoped he would not lose it. In early April, four weeks after his feet froze high up on the mountain, Marshall amputated a big toe that was threatened with gangrene. It would be early June before Brocklehurst could routinely get up for meals and short walks. In a gesture of compassion towards Brocklehurst, who had his 21st birthday on the slopes of Mount Erebus, and perhaps out of respect for him as an expedition sponsor, Shackleton gave over his cabin to the keen young baronet for several weeks after the operation. The bunk, though, was 'six inches too short & one cannot stretch one's legs'. The Boss might have had another reason for vacating his bunk and taking over Brocklehurst's bunk in the cubicle with Armytage. He was worried about his Australian pony handler. The 38-year-old seemed to be the least well adjusted to Antarctic isolation and needed reassuring about his value to the expedition. Armytage appeared depressed at times.

Through April, McMurdo Sound's short summer wore thin. Night hours began to exceed the daylight period. By 1 April it was dark by about 4 p.m.; on the 23rd they saw the sun set for the last time, just before a blizzard arrived. The sun would not return for four months. Although there would be daylight either side of noon for a while yet, the sun would not hit the Cape Royds headland again until 22 August.

Some fieldwork continued through the diminishing twilight and the increasing cold. Pony Lake's ice cover, which acquired the name Green Park, was good for exercising the ponies and dogs and for outdoor games, including hockey, football and rugby. Six times up and down the Green Park made a mile. Shackleton wrote: 'Our walks amongst the hills and across the frozen lakes were a great source of health and enjoyment.'

In early June, back in Regent Street, London, Shackleton's manager, Alfred Reid, was prompted, presumably by instructions left with him, to order more whisky for the relief voyage by *Nimrod* when summer arrived. On 10 June Reid wrote out an order for 12 cases of Mackinlay Scotch 'exactly as supplied to the Expedition last year', with each case labelled this time: 'British Antarctic Expedition 1907 s/y Nimrod Lyttelton New Zealand'.

Meanwhile, through the winter darkness at Cape Royds, inside the hut, the Mrs Sam range kept burning coal and seal blubber without pause.

13 —
SURVIVING
WINTER

I f Ernest Shackleton had been a party-pooper, he would not have gone to the trouble of ordering 24 dozen (288) Christmas crackers for the midwinter feast and other celebrations at Cape Royds. Back in England he'd known how important the winter solstice celebration would be for his cooped-up Antarcticans — a turning point of immense psychological import. After 22 June his men would look forward to the return journey of the sun into the Southern Hemisphere. Out with dark days and pessimism, in with the returning light and optimism. It would be a few weeks, however, before the first glimmer of daylight appeared around noon.

Shackleton had ordered two gross of crackers from the English firm that invented them, Tom Smith's of London. The basic model has remained the same for 150 years — a cardboard tube containing a party hat, a printed joke and some little knick-knacks, wrapped in brightly coloured paper with a twist at each end. When the twists are pulled, the cracker opens with a chemically induced bang and the contents tumble out.

Midwinter's Day 1908 was always going to be a big occasion in the life of the British Antarctic Expedition. On the eve, there were carols at midnight from an 'Antarctic choir' assembled in the porch, a surprise for those tucked-up in bed. The choristers, including Bernard Day in his pyjamas, sang half a dozen carols before the subzero cold got to them. Although someone suggested drinks all round, no party ensued.

The following day, sunless and starlit, was clear and considered relatively mild at minus 24 degrees Celsius. The ponies, now down to four, were taken on their usual morning exercise and the dogs allowed to run free. After lunch, a bath was poured close to the range, the source of everything hot, and the men took turns to clean themselves up and shave or trim beards. For some of the expedition team it was just their third bath since February. There was no afternoon tea that day.

So to the highlight of winter, starting at 6 p.m. . . . .

A feast. A time to be merry. A time to hear stories, listen to readings, exchange presents, sing songs, eat and imbibe. The dining table is laid with more finery than usual, including a printed souvenir menu that mixes haute cuisine with humour. Turtle soup is to be followed by an entrée selection of penguin patties and seal cutlets, with roast reindeer for the main course, accompanied by blackcurrant jelly, potatoes and green peas. For dessert there are Christmas specials: plum pudding, Ealing cake and mince pies. Coffee, cigars and cigarettes to finish. On the printed menu drink matches appear in the margin — whisky with soup, champagne to accompany the entrée, and whisky again for the main course and dessert. Anyone would think the printers, Wild and Joyce, had a hand in suggesting the drinks, and they surely garbled the last suggestion: 'MORE WHISHKY!!!!!?', which is printed

MENU.

Soup.

Whisky   Turtle.

Entree.

Champagne   Penguin Patties.
Champagne   Seal Cutlets.

Joint.

Whisky   Roast Reindeer and Black Currant Jelly.
Whisky   Potatoes.   Green Peas.

Sweet.

Whisky   Plum-pudding. Ealing Cake. Mince Pies.

Coffee. Cigars. Cigarettes.

ƧOⱮE WⅢISH ꓘY!!!!!?

Sledges at 12 - 30.

Menu for the midwinter
celebration, 23 June 1908.

with several letters sideways and upside down. There is a hint of Shackleton humour and restraint in the last line, 'Sledges at 12-30' — seemingly a Victorian echo to the party-goers, advising them of the time their 'carriages' would be ready to take them home to bed. The menu is couched in a four-page leaflet, with the pinkish cover carrying lines from Tennyson:

> *When the shadow of night's eternal wings*
> *Envelopes the gloomy whole,*
>
> *And the mutter of deep-mouth'd thunderings*
> *Shakes all the starless pole.*
> — from 'The Coach of Death'

A Marston line-drawing of the hut with a smoking Erebus as the backdrop leads to the menu, at the head of which is another Marston impression of the hut, this time in winter darkness. Its illuminated porch is a lonely beacon against the black rock and an aurora spreads curtains of light across the skyline. There is space on the last page for everyone's signature to make it a souvenir to cherish.

Cook Roberts has excelled himself by preparing a feast fit for explorers a long way from home. Strung up overhead and arrayed around the hut are the crackers. Most of the diners have dressed for the occasion, sporting a mixture of jackets and heavy woollen jumpers. Their dress suggests that not too far from the Mrs Sam range floor temperatures are close to freezing. Everyone's hair is neatly cut and combed. Most men are clean-shaven. Seated more or less in their cubicle pairings with the Boss at the head of the table, they tuck into several courses of food. At the end of the feast

Shackleton distributes tins of toffee contributed by his wife, Emily, and Christmas cards.

For the British-based members of the expedition, used to Christmas and winter solstice coinciding, it is easy enough to pretend it is Christmas. No one is going to mock or challenge them here. Indeed, the Nimrod Hut is what Shackleton calls their 'whole inhabited world', a capsule of light and warmth on the edge of the world's loneliest, least-known, last-discovered continent.

Prof David enters into the Christmas spirit by reading an excerpt from Charles Dickens's *A Christmas Carol.* The men put on paper hats after the crackers are pulled; there are masks and false noses, too. It is a relief to some of the diners that 'Putty' Marston has decided not to dress up as a woman again, complete with lipstick and rouge. He tried it once or twice earlier in the year, during daylight hours, to welcome home field parties — a stunt that had a mixed reception. Mackay, for one, did not find it funny. Marston also has a 'death's head' caricature that he presents to startling effect and can foot it wrestling Joyce, short and robust, in friendly combat.

There is plenty to drink. Mackinlay's Rare Old Highland Malt is a feature, and champagne is on the menu. Priestley, not partial to strong drink, will write in his diary that 'the duty was taken off alcohol with very fair effects'. Swilled from enamel mugs, the alcohol loosens tongues — and emotions. There is a singsong till midnight and the gramophone is hand-cranked and rewound time and again to enliven the party. Conviviality pervades the hut, no question, but there are underlying tensions and personality clashes.

Roommates Mackay and Roberts are at odds. The reasons for this are not obvious. It could be simply that the winter darkness and confinement has played on their minds and made small niggles seem outrageous. Scotsman Mackay slips off to bed soon after dinner is over, having consumed about two-thirds of a bottle of whisky in the opinion of Marshall, the expedition's senior medical officer. Eric Marshall has been quiet all evening at one end of the table, anticipating his rostered night watch, which begins at midnight. He has issues with the leadership. He sees faults in Shackleton, and records them in his diary. He believes Prof David has too much influence on the leader's decisions. The latest, smouldering issue is about a daring winter journey Marshall is proposing — to Cape Crozier, the eastern tip of Ross Island, to recover emperor penguin eggs for biological science — but the Boss, whom he mostly refers to as 'Shacks', 'Sh' or 'S—' in his diary entries, is not at all keen.[24] Shackleton believes a Crozier trip could jeopardise the South Pole journey. If the two events ended up overlapping, the more important Pole attempt would be delayed, perhaps fatally.

At midnight, when the singsong is halted, a few of the midwinter celebrants call it a night. Shackleton is among them. He disappears into his cubicle, perhaps feeling that the men might appreciate socialising without their leader present. The more serious drinkers continue partying, although their conversations can be heard in the bunkrooms.

By 1.30 a.m. Frank Wild, known for his whisky drinking and having followed the menu's directions, is in a drunken state and, according to nightwatchman Marshall, 'anxious to make a row'. Marshall, head and shoulders taller than Wild, manages eventually to get the storeman to go to bed, although for a moment the doctor's thoughts turn antagonistic: 'Was seriously thinking of getting him outside to give me a hand with

The midwinter feast at the Nimrod Hut, Cape Royds, in June 1908.
Ernest Shackleton is at the head of the table. On the left side are
Armytage, Brocklehurst, Marston, Day, Adams and Marshall; on
the right, Roberts, Mackay, Murray, Wild, Joyce, Mawson and David.
Missing is Raymond Priestley, who presumably took the photograph.
SCOTT POLAR RESEARCH INSTITUTE, REF P59/61/81

Music to breed by — George Marston, ever the prankster, playing
the gramophone at Cape Royds for nesting Adelie penguins.
THE HEART OF THE ANTARCTIC

the ponies,' he told his diary, '& then giving him a damned good hammering, as he was becoming very talkative and objectionable & Shacks was evidently afraid to come out and stop him, although wide awake and hearing all he said.'

Finally, by about 2 a.m., everyone is in bed; the solstice Christmas party is over.

The photograph chosen by Shackleton to depict the midwinter feast in his official record of the expedition, *The Heart of the Antarctic*, depicts a rather humourless crowd of men, sitting pale, shoulder-to-shoulder and unevenly illuminated by the overhead gaslights. Christmas crackers hang in sparkling profusion above the table. But there is hardly a bottle of strong drink to be seen on it. Lips are tight, expressions range from indifferent to glum, and no one is smoking. Was Shackleton trying to convey an atmosphere of restrained sobriety with this photograph, which he captioned, 'The Mid-Winter's Day Feast'? Compare this Cape Royds scene to the midwinter's party at the Cape Evans hut three years later, on Scott's Terra Nova expedition. Certainly there is a larger group at Cape Evans, but spread along the table are at least 16 bottles of wine and hard liquor lying empty or part-filled, and the mood is a lot brighter.

Photography was a popular hobby for the Nimrod expedition members. In addition to having on board an artist, Marston, who could work in pencil, oil, pastel or watercolours, Shackleton wanted the expedition to be well covered photographically. No fewer than 15 still cameras of different makes, a mixture of roll-film cameras and the bulky old dry-plate kind, were landed at Cape Royds. Shackleton bought nine of them for the expedition; the rest were privately owned. There was also a cine-camera, which Marshall operated. Drawbacks with Antarctic photography included the freezing of lubricants in the cameras, the brittleness that developed in roll film because of the low temperatures, and the need for a lot of water for the darkroom developing and fixing.

Shackleton had an outlet in mind for artworks, if not for photos, that were produced at Cape Royds — a home-grown publication, the first book printed in Antarctica. He had edited *The South Polar Times* magazine during the 1903 winter with the Discovery expedition. But printing a book in Antarctica was something else again. The London printers Joseph Causton & Sons provided a small lithographic printing press for the Nimrod expedition, the one now housed in the cubicle of Joyce and Wild. The pair had received three weeks' basic training from Causton's, which also donated paper, ink and type, and Marston had learnt the rudiments of etching and lithography, and had a hand in editing. Day, technically minded, was in charge of binding the book.

An indoor project to while away winter, the book involved nearly all members of the party either in writing contributions or in the printing and binding process. Ten articles were accepted for the book. Marston took on the job of designing and illustrating it. Shackleton was the overall editor, with Marston assisting.

There were technical issues. Dust from the coal range settled on the paper at times and the air in the hut was too cold for the printing press ink, making it tacky. To warm the ink, a candle was kept alight under the ink plate. There were issues with the lithographic processing of illustrations as well, but eventually Joyce and Wild set the press rolling. The book, 120 pages long, ended up with the title *Aurora Australis* — southern lights — after the shimmering pastel curtains visible in the heavens through the sunless months.[25]

The print run was small. Reports vary on just how many copies of the book were produced — up to 100.[26] Only about 70 can be accounted for today. Bernard Day worked hard on the binding, spending many hours sanding the plywood venesta boards smooth to make hard covers, and stitching each book by hand.

Among the miscellany of articles and poems was an unsigned essay titled 'Trials of a Messman'. It was written by Raymond Priestley in his witty style. Messman duties in support of cook Roberts were rostered. Apart from serving food, the duties included ice collection for the water supply, carting bags of coal inside, digging out frozen mutton from a snowdrift beside the hut, and sweeping the hut floor. He was 'expected to do everything and do it all at the same time . . . At nine o'clock I serve the porridge, distributing it about equally between the inside and the outside of the bowls.' With breakfast served, the messman would sit down to stone-cold porridge himself 'beneath a fire of criticisms'. The dining table was a curiosity, built of lids of cases, some of which still had their labels. One read: 'To be opened on Christmas Day'. Tea drinking habits merited a comment: 'The capacity for this expedition for tea is simply marvellous; some of the members take it in a bath; and among the many things I have learnt is that Scotchmen take more tea than "whuskie" (though that may be because they can get no "whuskie"), and that they are more particular about it than even Australians.' There was no accounting for taste when it came to additives: 'I have seen men spreading chutney on their bread and putting honey in their porridge, and, from the way it has disappeared, I have reason to believe that they take Worcestershire sauce with their fruit.' At clean-up time, there were ironies. 'It is a sight for the gods,' wrote Messman, 'to see a well-known F. R. S. [Fellow of the Royal Society] drying a wet plate with a wetter cloth and looking ruefully at the islands of grease remaining, after he has spent five minutes hard work on it.'

Dr Marshall, writing under the pen-name Lapsus Linguae (Latin for 'slip of the tongue'), produced an entertaining, galloping jingle titled 'Southward Bound', which described the voyage south in 13 verses, including:

> *Watch by watch for two hours at a stretch*
> *to the pony stalls we clung,*

> *With the water knee-deep on the for'ard hatch,*
> *and the decks a-swimming with dung.*

And towards the end:

> *In a solitary hut on a lonely isle*
> *beneath a smoke capped height,*

> *Hemmed in by the ice that grips us awhile*
> *we wait in the long dark night.*

That long dark night had many enlightening moments, not the least the appearance of the book, a remarkable achievement given the environmental conditions and the technical hitches. For one thing, the inking roller had to be remade after it melted from too much candle power.

Then there were books, cases of them. Prof David had brought a whole set of Dickens novels and, with a passion, read from several of them through the sunless months, sometimes so late that Shackleton would remind the narrator and his audience that it was after one o'clock or whenever, and time all good explorers were in bed. The Boss had Shakespeare's comedies and Robert Browning's poetical works for personal enrichment, Adams had *Travels in France*, Murray a selection of magazines, and Marshall *The Bible in Spain* and *The Merchant of Venice*.[27] For reference, the *Encyclopædia Britannica* was on hand. Material about other expeditions included Darwin's *The Voyage of the Beagle* and a set of reports from Scott's Discovery expedition. Writing of personal diaries filled in a lot of hours.

Shackleton was determined to keep his men busy and entertained through the winter by implementing a 'steady routine' of household duties and scientific work, outdoor recreation with dogs and ponies whenever the weather was conducive, and plenty of indoor entertainment. The gramophone was a winner and seemed to be going most nights, definitely on the nights when strong drink was in the offing. Gramophones were newish, having become available commercially in the 1880s and 1890s. The supply of 78-rpm records at the hut included popular songs like 'Because', classical works and hymns. Scottish music-hall star Harry Lauder ('I Love a Lassie' and many other songs) was popular for a singalong session. Marston, Mackay and Wild were to the fore in the singing. They could belt out a medley of shanties (spelt 'chanties' then), work songs sung mostly by sailors, among them 'Blow the Man Down' and 'Whisky Johnnie'. The middle verse of the latter ran:

> *If whisky was a river and I was a duck,*
> *Whisky, Johnnie,*
>
> *I'd dive to the bottom and never come up,*
> *Whisky for my Johnnie.*

Non-singers might turn to other entertainment — card games such as poker and bridge, and the matador game with dominoes. Model-making was another consumer of recreational time through the months of darkness. Two models of *Nimrod* were constructed.

All in all, Shackleton's approach to winter fulfilment worked, allowing him to claim on his return: 'The spectre known as "polar ennui" never made its appearance.'

Laundering was not high on the list of things to do. If you could go a week without washing shirts or underclothing, you could go several weeks, months even. There was little time for it or space to dry the washing, and hot water was a precious commodity. James Murray took a philosophical stance on the subject. In a cheerfully frank account of expedition life, published in 1913 and titled *Antarctic Days*, Murray provided down-to-earth advice on how to always have a clean shirt:

> *With water scarce, wear one shirt till you think it's*
> *dirty, swap for a clean one and wear till it is less*
> *clean than the first, then change to the first one*
> *again and so on.*

Biologist Murray, who suffered from a chronic gastric illness at Cape Royds and did not go on long explorations, summed up Antarctic life as 'not all picnic but that term aptly describes life at the main camp with a crowd of good fellows'.

On a typical day in winter the hut interior would have been filled with comforting aromas from soups, roasts, pies, stews and bread coming from the coal range and kitchen, cigarette smoke and pipe tobacco, candles, the acetylene gas plant, clothes drying

Sledge repairs and maintenance inside the Nimrod Hut during winter, with Frank Wild prominent. Shackleton is second from left, at the back, alongside Priestley, and Adams is beside Wild, also smoking a pipe.
SCOTT POLAR RESEARCH INSTITUTE, REF P98/9/15

off, printer's ink, wax being rubbed into sledge runners, and lubricants applied to car parts that mechanic Day would choose to work on inside the hut on days too rugged for working outdoors. Not so salubrious was the scent of burnt Weddell seal blubber, which at times escaped the range and oozed across the adjacent floor. Merging with scoria brought in on the men's boots, the blubber made a fine old mess, reminding Murray of the environs of a whaling station.

When there were blizzards, and there were several before the sun returned, the hut shuddered so violently it seemed as if the next big gust might carry it off into the Antarctic night. But the wire-rope tie-downs and the fastenings kept faith with the expedition; the hut remained on its frozen foundations. During storms no one ventured outside unless on business or to brave the latrine.

In calmer weather, the dogs provided recreation, even though Shackleton had more or less decided not to use them on the South Pole trek or any of the longer journeys. Ponies, yes; dogs, no. Joyce was in charge of the dogs, their feeding and training, and had help from Priestley and Marshall in particular. Sometimes Joyce would be seen rolling on the ground while 'a crowd of huskies' frolicked on and around him.

Priestley reported bonhomie in fine measure, at least through the early stages of the long winter. His diary a month into the season was joyous: 'I have heard it said frequently on the way out here, that a well-managed Expedition was nothing but a glorified picnic with a spice of danger, and our stay here has certainly upheld, so far, the truth of the remark, for I never experienced as much pleasure & wild excitement when eating an out-door meal under a notice, "Trespassers will be prosecuted" as I have done here in living a very primitive life in a well-equipped Expedition.'

Of course, the long sledging journeys were yet to happen. Priestley also mentioned tensions among the men in his diary, including the 'huffy' state the youngest, Philip Brocklehurst, got into one afternoon in July. He had a row with Wild for some reason and 'caused a good deal of anxiety by clearing out alone for a couple of hours without telling anyone where he was going'. Brocklehurst returned from the dark outdoors an hour after tea, having walked off his niggle with Wild.

The end of July raced up. Temperatures reached new lows — minus 40 degrees Celsius (same in Fahrenheit) on 28 July. Three weeks later, on 19 August, meteorologist Adams measured minus 41.9 degrees Celsius (minus 43.5 degrees Fahrenheit). It was the lowest temperature of the entire expedition.

As a precaution against scurvy and to ensure maximum fitness and condition among the men for the hard yards coming up in spring, Marshall wanted fresh meat included in at least one meal daily. Fresh vegetables and fruit were unavailable, but fresh meat was thought at the time to combat scurvy. Vitamin C had not yet been identified as a frontline antiscorbutic agent.

Marshall was also conducting a round of medical check-ups with an eye on who was fit for a South Pole trek. Wild, considered the fittest of all despite his love of whisky, was a front runner — a relatively lightweight (69 kg) member of the team but resourceful and deserving of his 'hard man' image. Joyce, on the other hand, a drinking pal of Wild's, appeared to have liver weakness, and a poor pulse, according to the doctor. Joyce was not amused to be told this. Sir Philip Brocklehurst, despite his young age and amputated big toe, had been expecting to be selected after Shackleton's promising noises in England about joining a conquest of the Pole; but Marshall discovered cardiovascular issues — 'heart sounds weak'.

Adams checked out okay physically, although Marshall had reservations about his judgement and value in the field. Then there was 'Shacks', an automatic selection to lead the four-strong Pole team. 'Pulm[onary] systolic murmur still present,' Marshall noted, without knowing whether this would manifest on a marathon journey. Although the murmur might have been implicated in the illness that struck Shackleton on the Discovery Farthest South journey, Marshall did not say it would be a risk to the current Pole bid. Even after the invective he had dished up in his diary about the Boss, the doctor was maintaining a professional stance.

Three weeks later, however, the Marshall diary erupted again over an incident between 'Bobs' (Roberts) and Mackay, an aggravation of their querulous relationship. It seems that Roberts had teased or provoked the quick-tempered Mackay, who had responding by gripping his smaller roommate by the throat rather unplayfully. 'Shacks in a regular panic about it & threatens he will shoot him [Mackay]!' Marshall might have overstated the leader's reaction but concluded nonetheless that 'he is not to be trusted with a pistol'.[28]

There were at least four guns at Shackleton's disposal: a .45 revolver, a .32 revolver, a .303 rifle and a 12-gauge shotgun. None was required on this occasion. A week later, another ruction. Marshall accused the Boss of 'cowardice & unmanly behaviour' when he attacked a pup with a belt for some unidentified reason. The winter had gone on long enough.

Sunshine bathed Cape Royds for a few minutes on 19 August, a magnificent and uplifting day — the first sun they had seen in four months. It was no sooner up than it dipped below the northern·

skyline. Its return sparked a flurry of activity between spring blizzards, with the focus being a series of journeys to Hut Point to relay stores to the Discovery Hut for the push to the Pole.

Men were split into various combinations, sledging stores to Hut Point over the new season's sea ice with the aid of the car (as far as the Erebus Ice Tongue), ponies, dogs and manhauling. It was generally an overnight trip to Hut Point, with a camp at the ice tongue, and from Hut Point depots could be laid southwards across the Barrier at roughly 60-mile (96-kilometre) intervals along the route to the Pole.

August was still a very cold month, the sea-ice surface was rarely smooth-going and southerly gales could surprise parties exposed in McMurdo Sound. For the polar novices, this phase of the expedition was a good testing ground. On one of the Hut Point trips, Priestley was with Adams and Mackay. Priestley, who, like Shackleton, had had a teetotal, non-swearing upbringing in England, in the shelter of a Methodist family, recorded his objection to foul language from the expedition 2iC in particular:

> For three days we marched to a monotonous
> repetition of blasphemy every few steps from Adams,
> his favourite being 'Jesus f. . . . .g God Almighty!'.

Difficult ice or snow conditions could irritate anyone hauling a sledge who was feeling out of sorts. For Priestley it was a baptism into polar fieldwork he never forgot.

Through September the ferrying of stores south continued. Then on 20 September there was a farewell dinner to mark an intensified period of depot-laying and the start of a separate journey, almost as hazardous the Pole bid. This was the journey to locate the Magnetic South Pole on the ice cap northeast of Cape Royds, across on the continent proper. Some of the expedition members would not see each other until *Nimrod* returned to pick them all up. David, Mawson and Mackay were selected to go on this important mission, which would add kudos to the expedition in the event the Geographical South Pole was unattainable.

Wild and Joyce both had a good number of stiff drinks that evening, encouraged by Shackleton, it seems. Marshall later found Wild with a bottle of whisky that he had sneaked from the stores. The doctor had been given a kind of policing role by Shackleton when it came to alcohol consumption and promptly took the bottle from Wild, who acknowledged Marshall's authority by not complaining. According to Marshall, Wild had no recollection of the incident in the morning.

By the end of September the bulk of the stores going south had been ferried to Hut Point, and a week later Depot A on the Barrier had been built and stocked with maize and paraffin oil, 100 miles (160 kilometres) from Hut Point.

By mid-October the Northern Party were off and running on their unprecedented goal and the South Pole Party had been named: Shackleton, Adams, Wild and Marshall. They said goodbye to the remaining base members, including Murray and Roberts, on 29 October and set out south on what Wild called 'the Great Southern Journey'. Shackleton called it 'the long trail after 4 years of thought and work'.

They would be travelling unknown lands. The topography of the Trans-Antarctic Mountains and polar plateau beyond the Barrier, so well mapped today, was a mystery they were anxious to solve.

14 —
'THE LAST SPOT WORTH STRIVING FOR'

On 3 November, with four sledges bearing a total of 1.2 tonnes (2650 lb) of food and equipment and each sledge hauled by a pony, the South Pole Party and support team set out from Hut Point. Given the 1902 Farthest South expedition's struggle, they were late getting away and now they were in the hands of the weather, ice conditions, terrain and how well they could cope.

'Off for the great event,' wrote Marshall, and Shackleton put the venture into a global context: 'The last spot in the world that counts as worth striving for'. Shackleton wrote a letter to Emily that began, 'My own darling Sweeteyes and Wife', and was to be read only if he perished on the trek; '. . . remember that if I did wrong in going away from you and our children that it was not just selfishness . . . your husband will have died in one of the few great things left to be done.'

The consumables in the sledge loads contained meagre supplies of strong drink. There were small quantities of three liqueurs in two-ounce and four-ounce bottles — crème de menthe, orange curaçao and sloe gin (a red liqueur made from blackthorn berries). Whether any whisky or brandy was packed for medicinal purposes was not recorded. If Wild had slipped a silver hip flask of whisky into his personal kit he did not let on, although a hip flask was hardly a match for an expedition lasting three to four months. In fact, they would strive without much alcohol at all. The Pole four were lean and fit. Marshall, used to taking the weights of all expedition members on a monthly basis, had weighed them the night before — Shackleton 79 kg, Adams 73, Wild 69 and the doctor himself the heaviest of them at 89 kg.

From the first day they encountered debilitating soft or thinly crusted snow followed by days during which the ponies stumbled into crevasses. Blizzard winds slowed them as well.

After four days the support party turned back. The ponies were still going strong, although they were always fated to be on a one-way mission. Shackleton envisaged that fresh pony meat eaten at intervals along the way would stave off scurvy symptoms.

At camps they built snow walls as windbreaks for the ponies and covered them with blankets. Two standard polar tents comprised waterproof canvas wrapped around bamboo poles, with snow piled up on the skirt of a built-in groundsheet to anchor them. To avoid factions developing, Shackleton rotated the personnel around the tents. Cooking and snow melting was done on aluminium Primus stoves, started on methylated spirits and fuelled by paraffin. Their basic fare was 'hoosh', a thick soup with a selection of flavourings, pemmican cakes (dried meat and fat), Plasmon milk biscuit, cocoa and chocolate. They ate fresh seal meat in the early stages. The ponies were fed mainly a 'maujee' ration comprising dried beef and milk, carrots, sugar and currants.

On 9 November, towards evening, they were startled by a series of loud bangs, like the sound of big guns booming, coming from a long way off. Eruptions on Mount Erebus, perhaps, or the cracking of Barrier ice on the move.

Real gunfire ended Chinaman's life on 21 November. He had been struggling to keep up with the others. No amount of brandy would save him this time. The men built a snow wall to hide from the other ponies his instantaneous death, by a bullet — 'a merciful release' was how Eric Marshall described it. Wild and the doctor skinned him and cut most of the meat from the pony's carcass, depositing 36 kg (80 lb) and loading nearly as much again on the sledges for the men to consume in the next week or so. They found the meat 'a bit tough' on first try. A few days later, Marshall reported lunching on 'raw, semi-frozen horse flesh dipped in fat ... not very filling or pleasant but when hungry does not come amiss'.

On 26 November they passed a milestone: Scott's Farthest South. It was a stellar moment. With their fitness holding and three ponies still pulling sledges, they would exceed the record by a long way, the Geographic South Pole their ultimate reward. They were at latitude 82 degrees 18 minutes south. 'A day to remember,' Shackleton wrote in his log of the trek. The four new record-holders shared a four-ounce bottle of the Caribbean liqueur, orange curaçao. An ounce each and a toast to good health. 'Excellent spirits,' an unusually buoyant Marshall noted.

By now they were well down the Ross Ice Shelf opposite Shackleton Inlet, a deep right-angle incision in the Trans-Antarctic Mountains, which were trending southeast, still backbone rigid. The men and their ponies were tracking parallel to this section of the lofty range, never before seen by humans, and standing well away from it. They wanted to avoid the massive pressure waves,

The Southern Party set off into the great white unknown.
THE HEART OF THE ANTARCTIC

broken ice and crevasses that glaciers spilling onto the ice shelf from the plateau are liable to generate. By now, too, the plodding over an unvarying plain was akin to a treadmill experience. It took days to get up to a distant peak and pass it.

Shackleton's thoughts would turn philosophical: 'As the days wore on, and mountain after mountain came into view, grimly majestic, the consciousness of our insignificance seemed to grow upon us. We were but tiny black specks crawling slowly and painfully across the white plain, and bending our puny strength to the task of wresting from nature secrets preserved inviolate through all the ages.'

Concealed by the hard slog, the feelings of the men toward each other were expressed mainly through their journals. Whereas Wild had a code for his most extreme thoughts, about Adams he wrote: 'I pray daily that Adams may be struck dumb. His incessant idiotic chatter would make a saint curse.' Wild thought that Joyce and Marston would have been 'more use' as sledging companions than Adams or Marshall.

The ponies were a continual concern. Marshall wrote on 28 November: 'Noble little Grisi was shot (by me) tonight. He had worked faithfully and pluckily, never refusing . . . the last few days had been feeling badly so had gone off in condition.' The doctor, who knew the ponies well, felt that Grisi had been suffering from snow-blindness. They made a depot of his meat for the return journey and packed some for immediate use. They would eat it cooked or raw.

During a spell of calm, sunny days and in lifting temperatures they walked in shirt and singlet, taking turns in harness to help the remaining two ponies, Quan and Socks, pull the two sledges. But Quan was weak and shaky, almost out on his feet. At the

1 December camp, he was shot, delivering five days' meat to the men he had worked for all year. Now the manhauling began in earnest, with the four men harnessed to one sledge and Socks pulling the other. He whinnied pitifully for his lost comrades.

The next day they altered course, swinging right, due south, to intersect with the great arc of mountain ranges in the hope of finding a route through it. Through luck or 'Providence', as Shackleton preferred to call it, they happened upon a glacier of stupendous proportions, its marker a reddish mountain appropriately named Mount Hope. Wrote Wild: 'We could see over 100 miles of its length.' Marshall dubbed it the 'Golden Gateway'. It had a mesmerising effect. Wrote Marshall: 'All transfixed with wonder & joy at finding a great inland sea of ice stretching as far as eye could see & flanked by magnificent mountains.' He guessed it might be the world's largest. This was the Great Glacier, later named the Beardmore after their Scottish sponsor. It was close to 200 kilometres long, their route to the Pole.[29] At last they were off the ice shelf and heading inland — towards, in Marshall's words, 'the promised land'.

Through soft snow, crevasse fields, blue ice and granite rubble they climbed. On 7 December they camped in a crevassed area where the narrow ice slots and chasms, created by glacial movement, were disguised by a thick snow cover. You could sometimes spot a crevasse by a concave shape in the snow cover. But not here.

Picture this: The four men and a pony, with two sledges, have lunched somewhere in the middle of the Great Glacier, the epitome of Antarctic wilderness. They set off again. Wild is following the others, leading Socks with his sledge. After about an hour's climbing there is a shrill cry from Wild. The others look around.

There is no sign of the pony or sledge but Marshall can see Wild is in trouble. He is half down a slot. His companions rush to his aid. Wild is helped from the edge of a 'terrible abyss', a deep and silent darkness that has swallowed the pony whole but thankfully not Wild. He is 'deadly pale'. The sledge is snagged near the top of the crevasse, damaged at the front end but still operable.

Wild and the sledge would have been lost forever along with Socks but for a freakish piece of luck. As the pony toppled into the crevasse, its swingletree, a wooden crossbar to which the harness is attached, broke and released him. Otherwise Wild and the sledge would have been dragged into the abyss. At the time Wild had the reins wrapped around his gloved right hand and as the crevasse opened up, the glove slipped off, releasing him from attachment to the plunging pony.

Shackleton might have pictured Providence intervening yet again. He used the term frequently enough for his men to abbreviate it to 'Provy' or 'Prov' in conversation and in their diary entries. It had heavenly connotations, as if a higher power were orchestrating earthly matters. 'Provy' was Shackleton's creed, according to Marshall: 'What cannot be planned or foreseen is in the hands of "Provy"; Marshall wrote. 'Risks must be taken, but they are part of the daily routine, and if you live and believe in your creed the word assumes its normal place in the vocabulary, and is meaningless.'

Crevasses continued to plague the explorers — 'hell holes' and many of them. The going got so tough they had to haul the sledges forward one at a time, at times with ropes, and managed to accomplish this on rations. The leftover pony food, maujee and maize, was welcome, but they went without full meals each day in order to feast at Christmas on double rations. Biscuits were in short supply, given how far they had to march. The upper part of the glacier was reckoned to be the halfway mark to the Pole from Ross Island. Summer solstice, the longest day, delivered 28 degrees of frost and they still had not reached the plateau.

They celebrated Christmas Day near the edge of the polar plateau at 9500 feet (2896 metres) above sea level at latitude 85 degrees 55 minutes south. Shackleton described their position as 'very far from all the world'. Even Ross Island was a long way behind them, about 620 miles, close to 1000 kilometres. For breakfast they enjoyed 'double wack hoosh', lunch was 'double wack cheese' and in the evening they prepared a blow-out meal of double maujee hoosh, boiled with pemmican, Oxo and biscuits, followed by a small plum pudding with a brandy dressing. Then came sweets, cocoa drinks, and cigars with crème-de-menthe liqueur in miniature bottles. The Beardmore had been tough, too tough, and there was more high-altitude travel to come. Marshall estimated they needed to average 14 miles (23 kilometres) a day for three weeks to reach the Pole — another 294 miles (466 kilometres). He was worried about the headaches caused by altitude, shortness of breath, lower body temperatures and the general weakness affecting the group.

On the first day of 1909, 12 months exactly since the tumultuous send-off from Lyttelton, they took stock: nine days' food left for the outward journey. In a diary entry, Wild put his and the party's position bluntly: 'Would not take it on again for five pounds a day. If we get to the Pole twill be sheer luck and we shall be luckier still to get back.' Wrote Marshall: 'Chances for Pole look bad.'

Their leader's head ached badly. Two days later, admitting the Pole was out of reach, they set a new objective — to get to within 100 miles of the Pole. They made a depot of return-journey food and paraffin oil and pushed on with one tent.

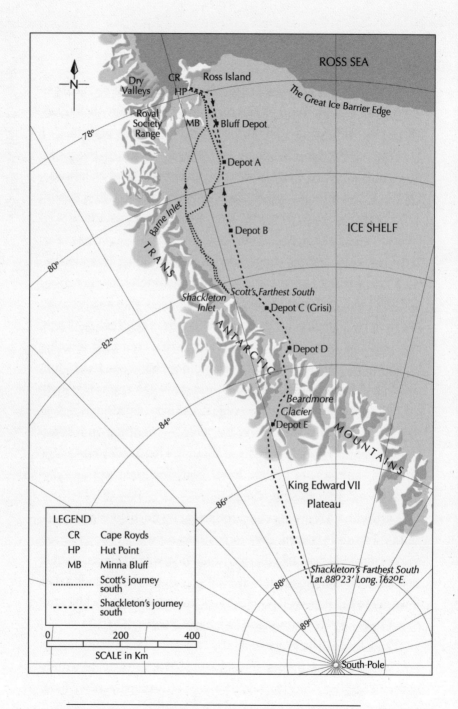

ROSS SEA

CR Ross Island

Dry Valleys

HP

The Great Ice Barrier Edge

Royal Society Range

MB Bluff Depot

78°

Depot A

Barne Inlet

ICE SHELF

80°

TRANS

Depot B

Shackleton Inlet

Scott's Farthest South

Depot C (Grisi)

82°

ANTARCTIC

Depot D

Beardmore Glacier

84°

Depot E

MOUNTAINS

King Edward VII Plateau

86°

LEGEND

CR   Cape Royds
HP   Hut Point
MB   Minna Bluff
.... Scott's journey south
‒ ‒ ‒ ‒ Shackleton's journey south

Shackleton's Farthest South
Lat.88°23' Long.162°E.

88°

89°

0   200   400

SCALE in Km

South Pole

The 1908–09 Southern Journey and Scott's Farthest South.
MAP BY ALLAN KYNASTON

A blizzard hit them on 7 January, much of which they spent in wet sleeping bags in the tent with no room to move, listening to Shackleton and Wild taking turns to read *The Merchant of Venice* and hoping the blizzard would not obliterate their tracks back to the plateau depot. Their feet froze. Wrote Shackleton: 'Every now and then one of our party's feet go, and the unfortunate beggar has to take his leg out of the sleeping-bag and have his frozen foot nursed into life again by placing it inside the shirt, against the skin, of his almost equally unfortunate neighbour.' It was to be their last camp on the outward journey. On 9 January they left the tent up, packed biscuits, chocolate and sugar and marched hard for five hours till 9 a.m., where, at latitude 88 degrees 23 minutes south (by dead reckoning), they declared a Farthest South record on a relentlessly high, cold and windy plateau, just 97 statute miles (156 kilometres) from the Pole proper. They hoisted the Union Jack, placed the brass cylinder containing the New Zealand postage stamps at the foot of it, and took possession of the plateau in the name of King Edward VII. Then Marshall lined up a photograph of the dismal scene — three near-faceless, hooded men and one oversized flag — and they promptly started backtracking.[30]

Adams, mostly a laconic workhorse throughout the journey, summed it up: 'If we'd gone one more hour we shouldn't have got back.' Wild, who had had misgivings about Shackleton through the winter months and even in the first month or so of the Pole trek, was changing his tune, describing his leader now as 'not such a - - as I thought'. He had seen Shackleton 'pull like the devil' and was now an admirer.

'We have shot our bolt,' wrote Shackleton, 'and the tale is 88.23 S. 162 E. . . . Homeward bound at last. Whatever regrets may be, we have done our best. Beaten the South Record by

The Southern Party's Farthest South,
January 1909. From left: Adams, Wild,
Shackleton; Marshall took the photograph.
CANTERBURY MUSEUM, REF 1940.193.189

366 miles [589 kilometres] the North by 77 miles [124 kilometres].'[31] In the history of heroic exploration, this was destined to become one of the most celebrated of all turning points. So near to their objective yet so far — and so desperate. That night they cheered themselves up with an extra dollop of pemmican washed down by the sloe gin liqueur.

Now for the return journey.

They found their last depot and made good time back to Depot E at the head of the Beardmore, covering 29 miles (47 kilometres) on one of the days at a trot with the assistance of tail winds and sail power, lessening altitude and warming temperatures. On 20 January they started the descent of the enormous glacier, dicing with death in crevasse fields. They all crashed though snow bridges at different times, saved by ropes and harnesses. Food ran short, and they were virtually out on their feet, starved and exhausted, before they made the glacier depot. After eight days they were at the Barrier ice, thankful, as Marshall reported, for 'many mercies', not the least fine weather. After worrying about the leader's condition on the way down, the doctor now reported: 'Shacks has stood it wonderfully.'

Soon Wild had an attack of diarrhoea and was unable to pull the sledge for a few days. By 3 February, the others were similarly stricken. Marshall blamed pony meat that had gone off in the warmer conditions: 'All laid up in camp with acute diarrhoea. Camp like a battlefield, some of us turned out 8–9 times in night.' For the next couple of days it would be a diet of biscuits and oats and counting every crumb. Their thinness was concerning.

Shackleton had his 35th birthday on 15 February between Depot B and Depot A. Depot B had given them the 'best feed for months', including a gravy they concocted using frozen blood dug up from where Chinaman had been shot and bled. The Boss celebrated with an extra cigarette from Depot B's stocks of smokes and tobacco, and everyone ate their fill of pemmican hoosh at the birthday dinner, along with luxuries like tinned sardines, cakes and crystallised fruit. No mention of alcohol. They were desperate now to make the 1 March deadline to meet *Nimrod*. It would be touch and go.

Five days later, Depot A brought them a top-up of food and the first distant views of Mount Erebus and Minna Bluff, the latter a waypoint in sight of Hut Point. It was a red-letter day, topped off by a pudding made of blackcurrants, biscuits and jam. 'Provy' had been kind.

On 25 February, a blizzard kept them tent-bound. Marshall went down with diarrhoea and collapsed while marching the next day. Shackleton, stronger now after the depot food and sensing the finish line, decided to leave the doctor and Adams at the camp, just over 50 kilometres from Hut Point, and trek there with Wild to organise a rescue party.

Shackleton's instructions, which he had left with Murray back at Cape Royds, were for *Nimrod* to leave for New Zealand on 1 March at the latest and for three men and extra supplies brought south by *Nimrod* to remain on Ross Island if the Southern Party failed to appear. Incredibly, as if knowing it might come down to this, he had requested that a search party set out from Hut Point on 25 February and that a continuous lookout be maintained on Observation Hill above Hut Point around that time for the men returning from the Pole. On the night of 28 February, the two oldest members of the Southern Party arrived at Discovery Hut. They were starving, exhausted and practically paralysed with cold from a blizzard and wind chill earlier in the day. Open water lay lapping

Eric Marshall at a camp on the return journey.
THE HEART OF THE ANTARCTIC

Hut Point but no ship was in sight. Attached to the hut was a polite but bleak note from Prof David. It stated that all other expedition members were safe and that *Nimrod* would remain in the vicinity of the Glacier Tongue (Erebus Ice Tongue) until 26 February. Were they two days too late? And what about his instructions to send out a search party and keep a lookout? Had they been ignored?

Finding no sign of life at the Discovery Hut 120 days after setting out, Wild wrote, 'We were past speech.' It seemed they had been given up for dead. But it was not in Shackleton's nature to give up. He tried lighting a fire with abandoned timber to attract attention, just in case *Nimrod* was still in McMurdo Sound, but could not get it started. He and Wild then cooked a makeshift meal and spent an uncomfortable night in the hut. Next morning *Nimrod*, with Captain Frederick Evans now in command and keen to escape a freezing-in of the ship, came steaming through frost smoke to Hut Point to land the wintering party, whose grim task it would be to locate four bodies. Instead, two forlorn figures were standing by the headland waving a flag — 'Provy' personified.

Through the next day Shackleton, resembling now a man with energy to burn, led a team back on to the ice shelf to rescue Adams and Marshall. It did not include Wild as the Boss wanted fresh legs with him. If Shackleton had been concerned before the Pole quest that Wild had a problem with strong drink, the Pole trek showed that his storeman and sledging partner could manage heroically without it. By 1 a.m. on 4 March all were on board *Nimrod*. The weathered, bewhiskered faces of the four Pole hopefuls, photographed aboard *Nimrod* that day, speak of incomprehensible hardship. They look like old men, having walked 2700 kilometres through the world's most challenging landscape at an average of 22 kilometres a day over 120 days.

They had traversed the largest known glacier and gone farther south than anyone in history. They had seen the heart of Antarctica, faced their own mortality, and perhaps even looked inside their souls.

As for the quest to reach that other pole, the Magnetic South Pole, Prof David, Mawson and Mackay were only too ready to relate their success — a sledging journey, manhauling all the way, of 2027 kilometres (1260 miles) in 122 days.

After leaving Cape Royds in the first week of October they had crossed the sea ice of McMurdo Sound and made their way up the mainland coast for about 250 kilometres, as far as the Drygalski Ice Barrier, before angling inland on a northeast track across the great ice cap. James Clark Ross, 67 years earlier, had realised that the Magnetic South Pole was well inland and out of the reach of his ships. Like their Geographic South Pole colleagues, they suffered life-threatening food shortages; frostbite, too. But they had reached a point on the plateau, no different at the surface from any other place, that their instruments told them was the magnetic pole — latitude 72 degrees 15 minutes south, longitude 155 degrees 16 minutes east.[32]

On 16 January, at an altitude of 2213 metres (7260 feet) they hoisted the Union Jack and gave three cheers for the King. They photographed themselves at this spot, since discovered to be not quite the right spot, then quickly left. That night back at their tent they celebrated with 'a little cocoa, a biscuit and a small lump of chocolate' rather than with strong drink. Back at the coast, dog-tired, reliant on penguins and seals for food and fearing they were marooned, the trio heard a shot ring out one day in the last week of January. It was *Nimrod*, their little ship. She seemed 'as luxurious as an ocean liner' to Prof David, who had suffered physically and

mentally on the trek back to the coast. 'To find oneself seated once more in a comfortable chair, and to be served new-made bread, fresh butter, cake and tea, was Elysium.'

Meanwhile, another three-man party comprising Priestley, Brocklehurst and Armytage spent two months in the glaciated mountain valleys west of McMurdo Sound, discovering more about the landforms, rocks and glaciers of the Dry Valleys region. *Nimrod* picked up the three men in the first week of February and heard another tale of a narrow escape — how the three men had been stranded for a time on an ice floe.

With the Southern Party now also safely on board, *Nimrod* went around the corner from Hut Point to Pram Point (the present-day site of New Zealand's Antarctic station, Scott Base) to collect a sledge, tent and geological specimens that came from the Beardmore Glacier area. The sea at Pram Point and elsewhere in McMurdo Sound was becoming cloudy and slushy at the surface. Sea ice was forming, a fascinating process of liquid transforming to a solid state. But menacing for any ship. *Nimrod* made for Cape Royds and its last pick-up — some personal gear, an anchor and a small boat left at Backdoor Bay.

An unfavourable wind, however, forced the ship to maintain her north heading. For Captain Evans the exit from McMurdo Sound could not come soon enough. His ship was already crunching through thin, curly-edged plates of pancake ice and nudging larger floes. As *Nimrod* passed the cape and the little expedition hut faded from view, the ship's company bellowed three cheers and sang 'Auld Lang Syne'.

Wrote Shackleton, nostalgically, clearly wanting to put the best face on the social side at the hut: 'We had been a very happy little party within its walls, and often when we were far away from even its measure of civilisation it had been the Mecca of all our hopes and dreams . . . I left at the winter quarters on Cape Royds a supply of stores sufficient to last fifteen men for one year . . . The hut was locked and the key hung up outside where it would be easily found . . . stores left in the hut included oil, flour, jams, dried vegetables, plasmon biscuits, pemmican, matches and various tinned meats, as well as tea, cocoa, and necessary articles of equipment . . . everything required to sustain life.'

No mention of stocks of whisky or other liquor. No mention, either, whether any of the 12 cases of Mackinlay's Scotch ordered in mid-1908 for the relief voyage had been dropped off at the now-abandoned hut.

Shackleton aboard *Nimrod* after the harrowing Southern Journey, March 1909.

ANTARCTIC DAYS, COURTESY DUNEDIN PUBLIC LIBRARY

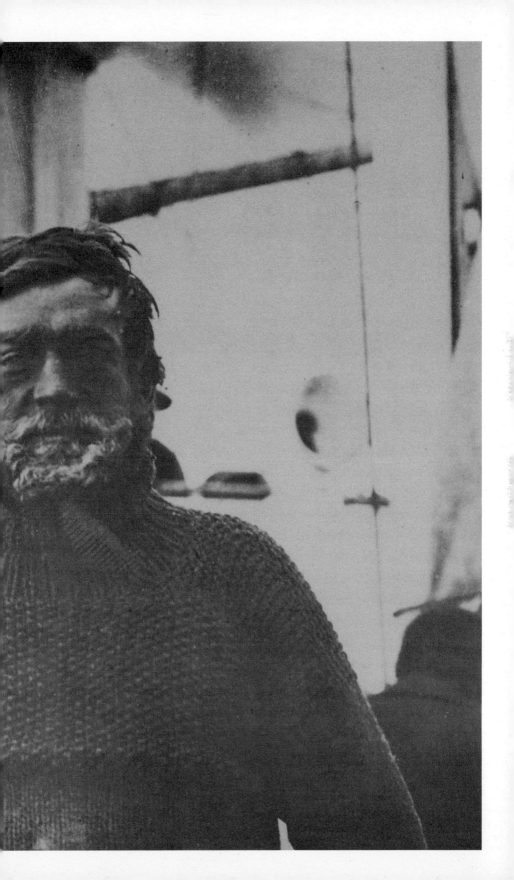

15 —
HOMEWARD

Biologist James Murray, the oldest of the five members of
the expedition who remained at the hut through summer
(Roberts, Joyce, Day and Marston were the others), recalled
how the return of *Nimrod* to McMurdo Sound in January 1909
was an anticlimax, pure and simple — 'more like an unexpected
douse of cold water than the joyful event we had so long looked
forward to'. Anyone who has wintered in Antarctica and longed
for a passage home during the dark months will know the feeling.
By the time the plane or ship arrives to uplift them, the winter
blues are over, the sun has returned and life is good.

Nimrod brought fresh supplies, although one sledge loaded
up with food and other provisions was swept away on a rogue ice
floe. The stores ordered for the relief voyage included Order No.
91 of 10 June 1908 under the letterhead of the British Antarctic
Expedition and directed to the Mackinlay whisky company. It was
signed by the manager, Alfred Reid. The handwritten order read:
'12 (twelve) cases Scotch Whisky in bond exactly same as supplied
to the Expedition last year'. In the left-hand margin of the order,
underlined, were two telling words: 'Medical Comforts'.

It is not clear whether, in the scramble to pick up three

A wall of packing-case shelving inside the Nimrod Hut, 2003, filled with items left by the expedition.
ADAM WILD

Cape Royds, from the air in early summer, 1962. Much of the headland's coast and hinterland is free of snow in summer, although the lakes retain most of their ice cover. The sea ice has broken out (bottom left) about halfway along the wider Cape Royds coastline and all the intact sea ice to the right will likely break out as summer proceeds.

ANTARCTIC DIVISION DSIR, COURTESY OF EUAN YOUNG

New Zealand biologist Rowley Taylor by the coal range in the Nimrod Hut, 1959.
ERIC WEDGEWOOD

The reindeer-pelt sleeping bag in Shackleton's cabin, 1962.
FRANK GRAVESON

Interior of Shackleton's hut in 2009.
LIZZIE MEEK/ANTARCTIC HERITAGE TRUST

The Nimrod Hut interior, 1957, reflecting the hurried departure of the last members of the 1907 British Antarctic Expedition in March 1909. Ice covers some objects.
ANTARCTIC DIVISION, DSIR

Donald Mackinlay, retired blender for the Mackinlay company, with the empty bottle collected from the Nimrod Hut in late 1956 by a United States Navy officer.
NEVILLE PEAT

sledging parties from three different locations, one of which had turned up days late, *Nimrod* managed to land any of the 12 cases of Rare Old Highland Malt Whisky at Cape Royds or Hut Point. In the event of a marooning on Ross Island of some members of the shore party, a case or two of whisky would have surely constituted 'medical comfort'.

What did go to their heads and their senses was reconnection with a green world. Their landfall in New Zealand was Stewart Island, the smallest of the three main islands and by far the most forested and least modified. When *Nimrod* pulled into the tidal inlet of Lords River on the island's east coast, where the forest is jungle-dense with tall trees, ferns and vines and kiwi calling in the night, the BAE members were overjoyed. The men scampered on a sandy beach with child-like excitement.

Shackleton decided to pull into lonely Lords River overnight in order to time *Nimrod*'s arrival at Halfmoon Bay, the island's main village, the next morning. Ever aware of how to manage public relations and publicity, he had promised the London *Daily Mail* first news about the expedition's achievements, which he now sent by Morse telegraph from the Halfmoon Bay Post Office. By the time *Nimrod* reached Lyttelton, Shackleton and his men were heroes. There were guns firing as *Nimrod* came up Lyttelton Harbour with an escort of steamers crowded with cheering fans, and many more people lined the wharves waving flags. Shackleton stayed in New Zealand for three weeks, enjoying a rapturous reception everywhere he went and astounding and charming men and women alike with his personality and his tales of adventure and endurance at the frozen end of the earth. The adulation continued in Australia; then he returned to England, more limelight and massive crowds — a picture of polar success. He was summoned to Buckingham Palace for an audience with King Edward VII and Queen Alexandra, who bestowed on him the rank of Commander of the Royal Victorian Order. To judge by the publicity and interest in his lectures, he could have planted the Queen's Union Jack at the South Pole proper instead of 97 miles short of it. In December that year he was knighted. Arise, Sir Ernest Shackleton.

In exploration and science, the British Antarctic Expedition had pushed boundaries: a new Farthest South and a new route to the Geographic South Pole, the Magnetic South Pole, the summit of Mount Erebus, and some scientific discoveries in the coldest place on the planet, including coal and plant fossils near the head of the Beardmore Glacier. There were lower-profile achievements, too. Scurvy never bothered any of the long-distance sledging parties. Said Shackleton in his expedition story, *The Heart of the Antarctic* (published in November 1909, five months after he arrived back in England): 'We had not one case of sickness attributable directly or indirectly to the foods we had brought with us.' Dr Marshall's insistence on fresh meat before the Southern Journey and during it appeared to have helped fend off scurvy symptoms. The Nimrod shore party sustained few injuries (Mackintosh's excised eye, Brocklehurst's amputated toe, Day's fractured foot) and, best of all, no fatalities.

Shackleton was inclined to make light of his unique approach to risk assessment in the field. When asked by Emily how he had had the strength of mind to turn back on the polar plateau short of the South Pole, he said he thought she would rather have a live donkey than a dead lion.

He had run risks financially, however. His expedition had cost at least £44,000 (a multimillion-dollar enterprise 100 years on) and he remained deeply in debt. After his return to England, the

British government donated £20,000 towards the expedition costs. Although this helped keep him solvent, he knew he would need more money still. As friend and biographer Harold Begbie said of his fundraising lectures, it was 'a case of Ulysses going round with the hat', of needing money to pay for the last expedition while he contemplated the next. For Shackleton was not finished with the Antarctic — not yet.

16 —
CAPE ROYDS
REVISITED

In September 1909, three months after Shackleton returned to England amid accolades and hero worship, Captain Robert Falcon Scott RN announced plans for another British expedition to Antarctica, and another pitch at the South Pole. This would be Scott's second expedition. It would end in tragedy. Like Shackleton, Scott had to stay flexible as to where to site the expedition hut when his vessel, *Terra Nova*, a 700-tonne coal-burning vessel converted from whaler to polar expedition ship, approached Ross Island in January 1911. Fast ice scotched his first choice, Cape Crozier, the eastern headland of Ross Island, and sea ice his second, Hut Point. So a gentle slope of scoria above the beach at Cape Evans became the base for the Terra Nova expedition, 11 kilometres south of the Nimrod Hut at Cape Royds.

Within days of their arrival, a group of five men ventured north over the Barne Glacier to Cape Royds to check out Shackleton's BAE hut. Among them was the expedition's 31-year-old senior geologist, Griffith Taylor, who had studied under Prof David at the University of Sydney. Taylor found a letter hanging on the inner door of the Nimrod Hut's porch (the outer door had been carried away, presumably in a storm). He recognised Prof David's handwriting on the envelope: 'To Any One who may visit Cape Royds'. The letter inside described the expedition's achievements in case *Nimrod* did not reach New Zealand with the news.

Locked up for just under two years, the hut interior appeared as if it had been abandoned the day before. Recalled Taylor: 'On the low table in the centre a meal [tongue, still in perfect condition] had been left. Condensed milk, saucers, biscuits, jam and gingerbread . . . At the back was a tray from the oven with a batch of scones just cooked, and a loaf of bread. The hut's last inhabitants had left in a hurry, which accounted for the somewhat unkempt appearance of the hut. Boots were scattered on the floor, books over the bunks, socks drying on lines.'

The visitors helped themselves to items from 'a huge store of unused food in one corner'. Taylor reported that the lunch they had before they returned to Cape Evans was 'a queer meal'. It included bacon and ship's biscuits (which they had brought from the Terra Nova Hut), corned beef, sardines, plum pudding, preserved ginger and bottled gooseberries.

Later in January, a party of three, including Raymond Priestley, made a visit to Cape Royds from Cape Evans in search of a stove for their own hut. Shackleton had brought a portable stove on legs to Cape Evans in 1908. Recruited by Scott as a geologist and now aged 24, Priestley had a strong sense of déjà vu: 'It was very funny to see everything lying about just as we had left it, in that last rush to get off in the lull of the blizzard. Nothing has been disturbed . . . some of the [bread] rolls showed the impression of bites given to them in 1909 . . . a half-opened tin of gingerbreads was a witness to the drying of the climate for they were still crisp as the day they were opened.'

Century-old bottled gherkins and onions.
ADAM WILD

Priestley thought the hut 'very eerie', as if still lived in. He and his mates spent the night in it. Wrote Priestley: 'I could have sworn I heard people shouting to each other.' In the morning, one of his companions, Victor Campbell, asked Priestley if he had heard any shouting in the night because he certainly had! There were several visits to the Nimrod Hut by Scott's men during the winter, and Priestley was back there again in December, leading a six-strong party on the second ascent of Mount Erebus.

The next expedition to visit Cape Royds — the last of the 'heroic era' — was that of the Ross Sea Party of Sir Ernest Shackleton's ambitious Imperial Trans-Antarctic Expedition of 1914–17. The role of the Ross Sea men was to lay depots towards the South Pole in support of the trans-Antarctic trekkers on their glorious crossing of the continent. But it all went terribly wrong. The main party's vessel, *Endurance*, was destroyed in ice on the other side of Antarctica. Led by Shackleton and the captain of the *Endurance*, New Zealander Frank Worsley, all 28 men took to the ice with boats, tents and provisions and drifted slowly north to the open sea, from where they reached a small piece of frozen, desolate and uninhabited land, Elephant Island. The nearest help was 1290 kilometres away at South Georgia, to where Shackleton, Worsley and four others sailed in the *James Caird* — a miraculous small-boat voyage that led to the rescue of the Elephant Island castaways.

Unaware of the loss of the *Endurance* and the aborting of the trans-Antarctic crossing, the Ross Sea men stoically and tragically laid the depots through two summer seasons.

In May 1915, their ship, *Aurora*, disappeared on them — swept out with sea ice from Cape Evans in a southerly storm. It would be nearly 20 months before *Aurora* returned to Cape Evans. The marooned men, left with little food, clothing and fuel, ate seals, burnt blubber and seized what supplies they could find at Cape Royds and Hut Point. Their leader, Lieutenant Aeneas Mackintosh, who had lost an eye serving with *Nimrod*, and Ernest Joyce, the Ross Sea Party's sledging expert and dog handler, were both familiar with the hut at Cape Royds. They knew its food stocks could be a godsend.

Joyce made the Nimrod Hut his home for almost three months in the spring of 1916. He went there with Irvine Gaze and Ernest Wild (brother of Frank). Gaze and Wild returned to Cape Evans after a few weeks. Alone at Royds, Joyce turned his attention to penguins, noting the arrival of the first Adelies of the season in early October. Any emperor penguins walking past Cape Royds were fair game to him. 'I killed and skinned 50 Emperor penguins for zoological collection,' he wrote. They went out with him on the relief voyage. At some point during his solitary stay he scrawled a sign on an old packing case inside the hut. It read, 'Joyce's Skining [*sic*] Academy'. He admitted afterwards: 'I became weary of my own company.'

Whether Joyce, a keen whisky drinker, enjoyed more than a wee dram at Cape Royds during those days of 24-hour daylight is not known. He would not have lacked the time and opportunity. But did he bother looking under the hut?

Shackleton, meanwhile, was immersed in a life-and-death drama of his own on the other side of the continent, performing miracles to save all of his expedition team as well as the officers and crew of the *Endurance*. Fresh from that ultra-heroic experience, which would make him a household name across the Western world, he made his way to New Zealand and Port Chalmers, Dunedin, where *Aurora* was being repaired and readied for the relief voyage. On 10 January 1917, she arrived back at Cape Evans to pick up the seven Ross Sea Party survivors, who were astonished to see Shackleton on board. They knew nothing of his Weddell Sea ordeal. Nor had he heard about the loss of three members of his support party.[33]

In the view of the survivors, Shackleton's arrival by sea from New Zealand was a less likely scenario than if he had trudged in from the South Pole, square-jawed against the elements and manhauling a sledge.

A week after *Aurora* nosed into McMurdo Sound, nervous of the sea ice, she set off on the return trip to New Zealand. The Boss would take his last look at the hut at Cape Royds, his only Antarctic foothold, where his 'very happy little party' had spent 14 months in 1908–09. He would not be back. No one would come near the Cape Royds hut for 30 years.

PART
3
THE
Match

17 —
THE ABANDONED
YEARS

F or three decades, the hut at Cape Royds was left to the Adelie penguins and scavenging skuas, as well as unconfirmed spectral entities and the more tangible elements — specifically, desiccating winds of diabolical force, blizzards, ice, permafrost and temperatures well below zero for much of the time. By and large, the hut's defences held. The roof stayed on. Wooden shutters on the south-facing windows fended off the ferocious gales from that direction. But each storm would blast the wallboards with scoria sand, snow and sea salt in summer and tear or chemically ablate a tiny fraction of wood fibre from the boards until the nails stood proud. Rust stains from the nails dribbled down the boards. During blizzards, snowflakes sought out the smallest cracks in the hut's cladding. The gaps were few. Any snowflake that did manage to penetrate the interior encountered a dark, calm, compatible environment. Ice crystals could survive here. The interior was virtually the same temperature as the air outside: below freezing point for all but a few days through summer.

Beyond the little hut, the lakes gained and lost ice cover according to the season, and the penguins, free of rampaging huskies and human egg collectors, doggedly raised their young at the physical and climatic limits of penguin breeding. If some nests were buried by heavy snow, the affected Adelies might nest somewhere more sheltered the next season. Over decades, the colony's shape changed, the abandoned areas looking like bald patches on the rocky headland.

In any one season a few penguins would waddle over to the hut, perhaps to prospect for a new nesting area or a new source of the coveted nest pebbles, Adelie 'bullion', or simply to satisfy curiosity. Some might wander over to moult in the garage or stables area. Guano built up and discarded feathers would fly under the hut in strong winds. A few curious penguins even climbed onto the bales around the stables — fodder for ponies long gone. Conspicuous in the nesting grounds on the Cape Royds headland were the remains of a 1907 wooden storage box. Presumably it had been blown there in a storm. Alternating as windbreak and nest box, it was a freakish object in the colony, almost as unlikely as a penguin turning up in the streets of central London. Since the year 2000 the crate has broken up, but its pieces are still visible — distinctive debris.

Besides the Adelies, Pony Lake and the hut area received occasional visits through the three decades from lumbering Weddell seals. For them it was a change from the sea ice. A crabeater seal might also have turned up — a species renowned for journeying far and fatally into the Dry Valleys on the other side of McMurdo Sound, there to become mummified by the intense, dry cold. On the sound itself, expressing almost organic intent, the sea ice maintained its annual cycle of birth, growth, dispersal and disappearance.

Inside the hut, on the other hand, change was imperceptible. The still, dry, freezing air slowed the processes of decay. No one came through the porch to rekindle the Mrs Sam stove, reignite the acetylene plant or light up a cigarette.

Beneath the floor of the Nimrod Hut, in the crawl space between the spruce boards (Shackleton called the timber 'stout fir') and the scoria ground cover, lay several cases of whisky and brandy that were nestled in the black volcanic sand with sundry supplies and equipment. In the dim world of the crawl space the cases were well protected from the sun's ultraviolet rays and wind damage. But blizzards could deposit small amounts of their frozen freight under the hut. The snowflakes sneaked in through the packing-case walls disturbed by the departing expedition team and through gaps in rocks or woodwork at the front of the hut. Snowflakes inherit the penetrative power of the parent water. They get in. Year by year, blizzard by blizzard, snow slowly collected around the cases and turned to ice. Sporadic melt-water floods in summer aided and abetted the development of solid ice under the hut. Such floods might occur in December or January as sun and daytime temperatures above zero melted snow accumulating as drifts against the hut walls. The melt-water would drain under the hut and some would refreeze at the end of the short summer.

This then was the scene for 30 years — the hut confronting the elements and seasonal wildlife at the edge of a frozen wilderness, the continent of Antarctica.

Given the near-continuous expedition activity of the early years of the 20th century, why did people not venture here between 1917 and 1947? For one thing, the South Pole had lost a good deal of its mystery for overland explorers, and there had been some disastrous setbacks, including the loss of Captain Scott and his polar party in 1912 and the failure of the first attempt at a trans-Antarctic crossing three years later, led by Shackleton, now Sir Ernest. Antarctic exploration, already a 'hard sell', was less appealing to sponsors, private, corporate or government. Then came the Great Depression of 1929, although world recession did not stop a well-heeled American explorer and aviator, Richard Evelyn Byrd, from mounting two Antarctic expeditions. A United States Navy commander, Byrd wanted to make his mark initially through aviation. He sought a reliable flat surface for take-off and landing. McMurdo Sound sea ice being dicey in summer, he opted to base his expedition on the Ross Ice Shelf, at Shackleton's Bay of Whales (also used by Amundsen as a base). With three others, Byrd flew from the Bay of Whales to the South Pole in November 1929. They were in the air for nearly 16 hours, and afterwards Byrd famously dismissed the Pole as a salient landmark: 'The center of a limitless plain,' he wrote. 'One gets there, and that is about all there is for the telling.' Norwegian whalers operated in the Ross Sea with factory ships and catchers in the 1920s and early 1930s, from a base at Stewart Island, but had no need to confront the McMurdo sea ice and had little interest in the land.

Politically, though, the ground moved. In August 1923, New Zealand formally took over British responsibility for administering the great wedge of Antarctica between longitudes 150 degrees west and 160 degrees east, due south of New Zealand. The sector encompassed the Ross Ice Shelf, McMurdo Sound, Ross Island, the Dry Valleys and a fair chunk of the Trans-Antarctic Mountains and ice cap all the way to the South Pole. This region, the southern gateway to the geographic South Pole and arguably the most interesting sector for earth and life sciences in all of Antarctica, became known as the Ross Dependency. The British flag had been raised in the Ross Dependency over and over again but New Zealand now had administrative oversight.

By this time the curtain had come down on the heroic era at the frozen ends of the Earth. Exploration on the grand scale of former times seemed a reckless waste of money — at least for the British.[34] In the next decade came portents of war then war itself, which developed into a black hole for resources and human lives. Interest in Antarctica bottomed out.

Following the war's end in 1945, Antarctica once more became a focus as countries with an historical stake in exploring the continent engaged in a surreptitious race for its resources and a rush for sovereignty. The Americans were the first out of the blocks. Towards the end of 1946 the United States Navy launched Operation High Jump with three task forces, 13 ships, 4700 personnel and more than 20 aircraft. Its operations south of New Zealand were centred on the Bay of Whales again. Flag-flying and coastal mapping were major imperatives, together with an interest in occupying the Geographic South Pole and all the time eyeing up the frozen continent's mineral resources. For the first time, ice-breakers with thick hulls of steel shaped like rugby footballs came crunching through the Ross Sea's pack ice and the sea ice closer to the continent. New Zealand took no part. Its government, absorbed by postwar priorities, expressed little interest in Antarctic activity.

United States Navy ice-breakers were the first vessels to penetrate McMurdo Sound since the departure of Shackleton's Ross Sea support party in 1917. On 20 February 1947, Operation High Jump's *Burton Island* came alongside sea ice off Cape Evans and shore parties were dispatched to check out Scott's two huts at Cape Evans and Hut Point. Solid ice partially filled both huts, limiting access. The following summer, under the banner of a smaller American expedition, nicknamed Operation Windmill, the ice-breaker USS *Edisto*, a sister of *Burton Island*, landed a party at Cape Royds by helicopter. They found the old garage and stables without a roof, and wall sections in a state of collapse.

Going inside the hut, the United States Navy men fingered and photographed old newspapers, magazines and nautical almanacs, and marvelled at the good condition of the 40-year-old foodstuffs and the bewildering array of expedition artefacts from an era that would have regarded a helicopter as techno-science fiction. Someone sampled maize from the hut that would later germinate back in the United States. There was talk about whether some members of the woefully deprived Shackleton support party based at Evans might have scavenged timber here for fuel. No one appears to have looked under the hut.

Never mind; the long siege of silence for the Nimrod Hut was over.

18 —
CARETAKING

Operation Deep Freeze, America's postwar thrust into Antarctica, was initiated in 1955. From offices in Washington DC and Christchurch, it established a permanent foothold for the United States in Antarctica — McMurdo Station at Hut Point. Destined to become the largest base on the continent, McMurdo Station was within an emperor penguin's trumpet call of Scott's Discovery Hut. Cape Royds had been investigated as a headquarters site and airstrip for the American base, but test drilling indicated too much ice beneath the volcanic material, so the engineers went south.

In the 1955–56 summer, helicopters from the Operation Deep Freeze ice-breakers called at Cape Royds on visits that were mostly recreational and 'sticky-beaking'. Some foodstuffs were removed 'for analysis'. Whereas most visitors came out a sense of reverence for a bygone era in exploration, some could not resist removing items from the hut and its surrounds. The Antarctic Treaty, international guardian of Antarctic heritage, had yet to be proposed let alone discussed, signed and ratified.

New Zealand mounted a national expedition in 1956–57, a year after the American initiative. Its government had been slow to commit to Antarctic activity, notwithstanding its stake in the Ross Dependency. It agreed to send a naval vessel, the research and support ship HMNZS *Endeavour*, only after persistent lobbying by enthusiastic members of the New Zealand Antarctic Society, a non-governmental organisation formed in 1933. There was a persuasive scientific carrot, however. The International Geophysical Year (IGY) of 1957–58 demanded some sort of New Zealand involvement.[35] Another prompt came from the British-led Commonwealth Trans-Antarctic Expedition by tractor-train, proposed for the summer 1957–58 summer. This expedition required a Ross Sea support party laying depots towards the South Pole, just as Shackleton had envisaged 40 years earlier. New Zealand accepted the role, and who better to lead it than Sir Edmund Hillary, conqueror of Mount Everest.

So HMNZS *Endeavour* was sent south early in 1957 and Scott Base was built at Pram Point on Hut Point Peninsula, three kilometres from (and out of sight of) the burgeoning American station. In the midst of expanding their own foothold on Antarctica, American naval personnel made a return visit to Shackleton's old base.

The following summer, 1957–58, *Endeavour* returned to McMurdo Sound and crewmen went ashore at Cape Evans and Cape Royds to undertake repairs and a 'spring cleaning' of the historic huts — the first tentative caretaking. At the Nimrod Hut the worn roof felting was replaced from a dump of original material and the *Endeavour*'s chief shipwright measured up for a new door for the porch. A metal plaque was fastened to the weatherboards near the entrance, declaring the hut's heritage value to visitors. Someone took a ham, cured and wrapped, back to Scott Base, where it was pronounced fit to eat and promptly placed on the lunch menu, to the delight of the IGY scientific team. 'Nothing wrong with it,' was the verdict.

The Nimrod and Terra Nova huts soon became VIP destinations on a regular basis, with the Operation Deep Freeze flights out of Christchurch in summer carrying hundreds of American and New Zealand expedition personnel and swags of dignitaries. Visitors' books at each hut filled up fast. It was clear the huts deserved more than haphazard maintenance. Systematic restoration was called for, and the loudest calls came from the stalwarts of the New Zealand Antarctic Society.

The government's response in 1959 — some would say a typical response — was to set up a committee. The Antarctic Huts Restoration Committee embraced the Antarctic Division and various other government and quasi-government agencies, as well as the New Zealand Antarctic Society. The society's long-standing president, Les Quartermain, a Wellington College history teacher, was appointed to lead a huts restoration party comprising members of the New Zealand Antarctic Society in the 1960–61 summer. Their focus would be the Nimrod and Terra Nova huts. The Discovery Hut, ice-filled, was less well endowed with artefacts than the other two, having never been occupied full-time by an expedition.

But this party of New Zealand volunteers was not the first to camp in or around Cape Royds. During the 1959–60 summer season, a 28-year-old technician from the Animal Ecology Section of New Zealand's Department of Scientific and Industrial Research made the place his home for four months. Rowley Taylor, who initiated the first New Zealand study of the Cape Royds Adelies, arrived there by dog sled on 23 October 1959 with the Scott Base cook and dog handler, Eric Wedgewood. There was no outer door to the hut and a large snowdrift adjacent to the porch became their freezer for fresh meat and vegetables as well as the source of their fresh water supply.

The hut interior was scarcely warmer. Seeking an area they could insulate, they chose Shackleton's cabin, moved bunks into it and erected a canvas 'door' and sailcloth ceiling from Nimrod expedition materials. Home comforts included a kerosene Tilley lamp (Shackleton's cabin had no window), a Primus cooker and a radio through which they spoke to Scott Base three times a week. Pinned up inside the hut — in the absence of a visitors' book — were notes from United States Navy personnel who had visited Cape Royds in recent years.

Without any coal to fuel the old stove, Taylor and Wedgewood kept wearing their balaclavas, eiderdown jackets and padded pants inside the main room. Collecting scraps of boxwood lying outside the hut, they tried lighting the stove a few times after making sure a fire would not set the whole hut alight. They would poke their stocking feet into the ovens. According to Taylor, the warmth was merely imaginary. Having read extensively on Shackleton in earlier years, he had immense regard for the explorer and the Nimrod expedition's achievements. But the hut was another story. Shackleton hoped it would 'provide harbour from the blizzards for those who come after'. Taylor's respect for the hut was simple: 'I considered it no different than any 50-year-old back country hut in New Zealand; to be used and carefully looked after for future inhabitants.'

With ample food supplies from Scott Base, Taylor and Wedgewood prepared nutritious meals and had little interest in what Shackleton had left on the shelves. Some pickles were opened and found to be acceptable, but the 50-year-old New Zealand

milk powder was awful. For a nightcap they would drink hot tea generously laced with overproof navy rum that Wedgewood had brought to Royds. They came across no alcohol in the hut, and the underfloor area was an iced-up no-go area.

Taylor's primary research interest was the Adelie penguin colony — the first intensive study at this southernmost penguin colony since the heroic era.[36] From mid-November, he was joined by another young New Zealand biologist, Euan Young, for the rest of the summer. A tall 23-year-old, Young had just completed a Master's degree in zoology at the University of Canterbury. He took over Wedgewood's bunk in Shackleton's cubicle and began studying the population of McCormick's skuas that arrived each year at Cape Royds, soon after the penguins. To Young, the hut felt like a small hall in rural New Zealand in winter — freezing: 'It was a perfect place for a field ecologist. There was no temptation to stay in it other than to cook and sleep.'

Young would later have misgivings about their use of the historic hut, the risk of fire being his main worry. Like Taylor, he was concerned about how helicopter engine and rotor noise was disturbing the penguins and skuas at Cape Royds and lobbied successfully for a more distant landing area. In the course of his studies Young discovered that skuas rely more on fishing at sea than on preying on penguins. Until then these Antarctic skuas were thought to depend on penguins for survival. Young returned to Ross Island through the 1960s to lead ongoing studies of the larger Adelie penguin colonies at Cape Bird.

At the end of December 1960 four hut restorers arrived at Cape Royds, well aware that Taylor and Young had been based there the previous summer. Led by Les Quartermain, the hut restoration team of 1960–61 spent 19 days at the cape, rebuilding elements of the hut and its appendages, sorting through stuff, especially the scattered heaps of packing cases, and giving the place a general 'spring-clean'. They scraped and scrubbed clean a thick coating of seal blubber from the floor beside the stove. Quartermain reported 'a scarcity of relics'.

His team worked on an inventory of Nimrod material, without a mention of cases of whisky or any other liquor beneath the floorboards. Numerous decaying items were consigned to the rubbish dump. Given Shackleton's intention to leave a hut worthy of a well-stocked castaway depot, how much had been removed in those first few years of human activity around McMurdo Sound? No one will ever know the full extent of the souveniring, but several items have been returned to New Zealand Antarctic authorities over the years, most from United States donors with a pricked conscience.

The 1960–61 restorers did their best to create a 'lived-in' appearance inside the Nimrod Hut, and topped off their work by re-covering the roof with tarpaulins and reinstating the tie-downs. They even made some discoveries, including parts of the Arrol-Johnston motor car. Over the next few summers, as hut restoration work continued, New Zealand-based biologists, including Bernard Stonehouse and Brian Reid, made fleeting use of the Cape Royds hut. Some would have known of the experience of Raymond Priestley and others 50 years earlier, and looked out for hair lifting on the back of their necks.

In the 1962–63 summer, Oliver Sutherland, a Canterbury University vertebrate ecology student, occupied Shackleton's hut for two and a half months and recorded the breeding success of the Adelie penguin colony, comprising some 2500 birds.[37] He was just 19. He arrived there with his lecturer and supervisor, Bernard

Stonehouse, who stayed 10 days, and from then on had the company, in turn, of Scott Base staff members, including surveyor Frank Graveson. Instead of basing himself in Shackleton's cabin, Sutherland opted for a living and cooking area in the corner of the hut formerly occupied by Prof David and Mawson, partitioning it with blankets. He and Stonehouse fashioned a table from an old door, and they slept in sleeping bags on Nimrod cots — until blizzard conditions arrived, that is. It grew so cold in their living space that for a time Sutherland was forced to use one of Shackleton's old reindeer sleeping bags as an outer cover for his New Zealand bag. Neither he nor his companions sampled the Nimrod Hut's food or drink, and they did not light the old stove.

For a time, Sutherland had the company of Scott Base information officer and budding author Graham Billing, and photographer Guy Mannering. They slept on improvised beds inside the hut. Billing based his compelling 1965 novel, *Forbush and the Penguins*, on the experience of a young New Zealand biologist studying the Adelies at Cape Royds on his own and coming to terms with solitude; intrusive visitors; nature in the raw, including the violence of Adelie penguins towards each other; and natural justice at large. It was promoted as the first novel to come out of Antarctica.[38]

After that summer season, camping in the hut by scientific parties doing summer-long studies ceased out of respect for both Nimrod expedition history and the restoration effort. From then on, the scientists and hut restorers would have to use a wannigan (an Alaskan name for a portable hut towed on skids) on their visits to Cape Royds or bring their own tents. The Mrs Sam stove could look forward to restorative treatment, more varnishing and a long retirement with its complement of pots, pans, grillers and earthenware crocks and in the company of three hams still hanging in the pantry alongside rows of canned and bottled food. Those seal-blubber days were well and truly a thing of the past, and the ghosts of the Nimrod Hut could rest easy.

Hut caretaking gained a new lease of life in 1970 following several seasons of inactivity. Through the government Antarctic office, New Zealand Antarctic Society (NZAS) volunteers — at the rate of a pair each year — were assigned to push on with caretaking. Canterbury NZAS members Peter Skellerup and Michael Orchard were the first pair. Tasks varied: reglazing windows, repairs to the cladding, removal of vestiges of snow and ice, restoration of artefacts. The hut caretakers were sleeves-rolled-up handymen bristling with Kiwi ingenuity. All of them were new chums. A criterion for their selection was no previous experience of Antarctic hut restoration. Every summer season through the 1970s a new pair of good keen men went south.

By now the Antarctic Treaty had been ratified by the 12 signatory nations, and more governments were signing up to the ideal of a continent dedicated to peace and science — no military shenanigans, and no disturbance or extraction of resources, including historic resources. Like diamond dust, the treaty sparkled with hope through the darkest days of the Cold War.

By 1980, the artisan hut-caretaker days had ended. With the advent of the Christchurch-based Antarctic Heritage Trust (AHT) in 1987 basic maintenance continued on an annual basis but this was a new era, involving corporate-lingo, and you had to have a vision, a mission statement, a strategic plan. The Antarctic Heritage Trust's vision was: 'Antarctic heritage: inspiring the future by conserving the legacy of discovery, adventure and endurance'. There was a Shackleton ring to it.[39]

New Zealand Antarctic personnel enjoy a hot-drink 'smoko' inside the Nimrod Hut in September 1963. They are gathered around a table in the corner of the hut that was the cubicle of David and Mawson. Packing cases at the top left show, partly obscured, an inscription by Ernest Joyce: 'Joyce's Skining [*sic*] Academy' — a reference to his penguin collecting in the spring of 1916. From left: Malcolm Ford (surveyor), Murray Smith (biologist), an unidentified United States Navy radioman, Frank Graveson (field assistant) and Barry Waters (carpenter).
MALCOLM FORD, COURTESY OF FRANK GRAVESON

A new century arrived, and with it the realisation that annual maintenance work by itself could not stem the processes of decay. A sea change in hut caretaking was required that would tap into professional expertise in science, engineering and conservation. Any kind of Antarctic activity did not come cheap; the trust faced fundraising on an unprecedented scale and looked overseas for support. The result of this major reassessment was the Ross Sea Heritage Restoration Project, launched on Ross Island in the summer of 2001–02 by Her Royal Highness Princess Anne.

There were four targets in this expanding scope of work in the Ross Dependency: Cape Royds, Cape Evans, Hut Point and Cape Adare in Northern Victoria Land (Borchgrevink's 1899 Southern Cross expedition wintering base). These places held Antarctica's first human dwellings. They were unique; so was Antarctica in terms of the history of human habitation. It was the only continent where the very first buildings still stood.

Through the trust's efforts and New Zealand's leadership, Cape Royds was elevated to the status of an Antarctic Specially Protected Area under the Antarctic Treaty system — officially, ASPA No. 27. It rubbed shoulders with another, older protected area, the Adelie penguin colony, designated a Site of Special Scientific Interest — SSSI No. 1, no less. Cape Royds resonates specialness, no question. Up to 2000 people a year get to visit, the majority from tour ships, the rest dropping in under the auspices of the New Zealand and United States Antarctic programmes.

First cab off the restoration rank, in terms of a conservation plan, was Shackleton's hut. The report was released in 2003, describing Shackleton's hut as 'an evocation of the heroic age of Antarctic exploration . . . The setting of the place is unaltered from Shackleton's time . . . The hut and associated artefacts are thus inextricably linked to the landscape, and together they define the spirit of the place.' Beyond the grand statements, the plan foreshadowed four years of intensive work, summer and winter. The programme aimed to arrest the decay and return the hut, 'as closely as possible', to its 1908–09 condition.

In addition to conservation work on the building's fabric, objects from inside and outside the hut received conservation treatment from teams of conservators working year round, with the winter team ensconced at Scott Base and processing objects sledged back to Pram Point and temporarily held in shipping containers there. During the summer season, from November to February, the main focus of restoration and conservation work would be carried out at Cape Royds. No objects were to leave Antarctica unless by government permit, a stipulation of Antarctic Treaty protocols. Heritage stuff had to stay in situ.

But heritage protection, at a sophisticated level, is expensive, and the Cape Royds budget was NZ$3 million. The New Zealand government stumped up about half a million dollars a year in baseline funding through its Ministry of Arts, Culture and Heritage. To fund the conservation work, the Antarctic Heritage Trust canvassed overseas for funds. British Antarctic interests, both public and private, were slow to respond. But in the United States, Shackleton was a modern inspiration thanks to a slew of new books and documentary films about him.

In support of the project's value was the timely listing of Shackleton's hut by the World Monuments Fund in New York — this little hut on the great white continent joined the world list of the 100 Most Endangered Sites. Donations rolled in. There were numerous big ones. The American Express Foundation World Monuments Fund put up US$100,000, and an anonymous New

York family contributed a similar sum. The Getty Foundation in Los Angeles donated more than once, its grants totalling US$350,000. Quark Expeditions, a specialist polar travel company, also donated to the restoration work. Every dollar went into frontline conservation effort.

Three years into the programme and following some public criticism from Sir Edmund Hillary and New Zealand prime minister Helen Clark, the British government put up £250,000, not for the Shackleton hut but for the next major exercise, the restoration of Scott's Cape Evans hut, a rather larger project than at Cape Royds. Compare this sum to the £154 quoted by the London manufacturers, Humphreys Ltd, in 1907 to supply a 'Portable House', 33 feet by 19 feet, in prefabricated form, to the British Antarctic Expedition. It was a wooden building, and nothing in the paperwork from the manufacturers hinted at the hut's life expectancy. The hut would be good for a year and beyond that, who would know or even begin to guess how long it might last? Which is why, 100 years on, the New Zealand stewards of Antarctic heritage turned to 21st-century science.

A collaboration unique in an Antarctic setting brought together the disciplines of microbiology, wood chemistry, biochemistry and molecular biology to study the impacts on the three Ross Island historic huts from the natural environment and introduced factors. Professor Roberta Farrell, of Waikato University's Department of Biological Sciences, and Professor Robert A. Blanchette, a microbiologist and expert in wood conservation from the University of Minnesota, were the team leaders, and the studies, which began in 1999, continued at least until 2012.

Not surprisingly, there were surprises. The studies discovered that living at the Nimrod Hut were some very unusual species of

A bottle near
the top of the
jemmied case
that was flown
to Christchurch
for thawing.

The iced-up whisky case with the
jemmied lid under Shackleton's hut.
ANTARCTIC HERITAGE TRUST

James Blake excavating
relics from underneath the
Nimrod Hut, January 2007.
NEVILLE PEAT

Lizzie Meek, Programme Manager Artefacts for the Antarctic Heritage Trust, at work on conserving straw-wrapped bottles of whisky soon after they were removed from the case at Canterbury Museum.

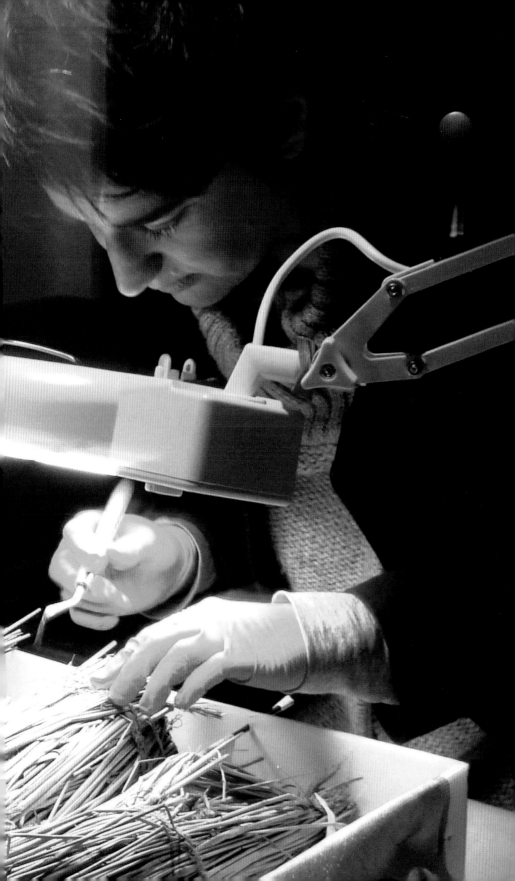

An original full bottle of
Mackinlay's whisky.
ANTARCTIC HERITAGE TRUST

soft-rot fungi (*Cadaphora*), which had taken up residence in wood near ground level. They were causing incipient decay. The fungi appeared to be encouraged by moisture from melt-water as well as from nutrients from penguin guano and feathers and the bales of pony fodder. The good news was that soft-rot damage to the hut and wooden artefacts and textiles was of 'no immediate threat'. But it ought to be treated. How? It was impossible to control these tough fungi with chemicals, and the use of toxic compounds would be prohibited in the historic structure anyway. So the conservators, with advice from the scientists, turned to environmental change to curb fungal growth by reducing moisture in and around the hut. This meant routinely clearing snowdrifts when possible and removing ice.

The rough, fuzzy appearance of external wood intrigued the scientists. It looked like mechanical abrasion but turned out to be chemical, manifesting as 'white to yellow-brown masses of detached fibres'. They call this defibration. It occurs when spray from ice-free sea hits the hut in storms, carrying traces of sodium chloride and other salts. Evaporation allows the salts to get to work on the lignin and other cellular components of the timber. When the door to the hut is open, the porch is vulnerable to defibration, trapping water vapour and salts. Visitors and AHT workers, too, unwittingly bring salts into the hut. You cannot be too careful when state-of-the-art scientific studies are monitoring things at microscopic level. In 2010, the collaboration extended to include archaeologists and conservation architects from New Zealand-based companies Geometria and Archifact who introduced high-resolution laser spectroscopy to look at the huts to micron level. This technology also helped gauge the damage from ultraviolet light, which in summer has a 24-hour window of opportunity.

Of more obvious concern is the spread of pollutants around all hut sites. Petroleum, asbestos and chemicals of various kinds were landed with the expeditions. High concentrations of hydrocarbons were identified in the scoria around the old fuel depots. A clean-up was initiated.

In 2004, the Antarctic Heritage Trust's restoration fieldwork started in earnest at Cape Royds. There were many pressing jobs. Replacing timber, waterproofing the building, re-covering the roof and repairs to the northern side of the hut — the stables, garage and latrine — were priorities, together with sorting through wooden cases, storage boxes, and individual items requiring treatment. Who knew what archaeological treasure might be uncovered?

Stores open to the elements along the southern and eastern sides of the building were carefully excavated and placed in conserved original venesta plywood boxes or placed in new timber boxes. A subterranean dam was built. Some wallboards needed repairing, and the roof's tie-down cables required realignment and tightening. A new outer door had to be made from timber equivalent to the original, with matching hardware and fixings — a challenging prescription that followed the 'like for like' replacement policy specified by the conservation plan.

The most exacting phase of the conservation work was conserving the individual, portable objects, estimated at 5000 in number. That grew to 6000 conserved objects during the course of the project. Items came from shelves and other parts of the hut's interior, from the 'jumble-yard' immediately surrounding the hut, and from various stores depots around the headland.

The conservation teams encountered the greatest environmental problems on the south and east walls of the hut, where many cases and their contents were in an advanced state of decay. Leaking cans, including some that were hazardous to the local wildlife, had to be treated or disposed of. Most of the objects were transported progressively to the conservators' work area at Scott Base in plastic 'cubers', which look like small dumpsters on skids. Trains of cubers would be towed over the sea ice to Scott Base by Hagglund tractors (all-terrain, amphibious tracked vehicles), there to be processed by multinational teams of conservators.[40]

A low-priority area in the search for objects was the space under the hut. It was a dark space, not easy to access. Much of it was choked with ice. In a no-man's-land continent, the crawl space seems to have been largely an expedition no-go area, a holding place for surplus miscellany. Perhaps a hiding place. It was the expedition's basement, where stuff could go missing. Or not be missed.

In the set of design drawings for the restoration of the Nimrod Hut, prepared by conservation architect Adam Wild and signed off in 2003, the drawings show the area of the hut's foundations as a blank space, marked: 'Ground level under floor undetermined'. This underfloor area has had a nebulous history and it was not surveyed at the time of the conservation plan assessment because it was largely inaccessible, with all but a couple of square metres of it at the southwest corner ice-filled.

In any case, with so much work to be done above the floor and all around the hut, interest in the basement space was minimal. Of more concern than hidden archaeological treasure was the ice itself, the extent of it and how it behaved. Ice under the floor was a threat to the restoration and structural integrity of the hut. During mild spells in summer it would typically glisten and melt

This iced-up whisky case recovered from under the Nimrod Hut
was destined for thawing at Canterbury Museum. The case is
thought to have been partly opened at Cape Royds during the
heroic era.
ANTARCTIC HERITAGE TRUST

then refreeze as temperatures fell. Melt-water raised humidity levels, and the higher the humidity the greater the risk to artefacts, woodwork and metal fastenings. Over time, pressure from the annual accumulation of ice could damage the floorboards. So to a remarkable discovery . . .

In January 2006, two seasons into the restoration, a member of a five-man carpentry team, Paul Terry, in the role of 'Manual Support', is assigned to have a go at removing the ice from under the floor — some of it at least, whatever is possible. It is strenuous, painstaking work, much of it carried out prone. Progress is slow. By the end of the season, he has removed about 40 per cent of the basement ice.

During his last few days at the ice-face there is a revelation: a couple of wooden crates show up within the ice.

Seemingly the size and shape of cases of liquor, they are more or less under Shackleton's 'cabin'. The labels, blurry inside their ice prison, suggest whisky cases. The words 'Rare' and 'Old' and 'Whisky' are just discernible. Terry and his colleagues wonder if the cases might contain full bottles of Scotch? If true, the whisky will be touching 100 years of age! Could this be the whisky find of the century?

19 —
THE COOLEST COOLROOM IN THE WORLD

Ice preserved the Mackinlay whisky in two senses. First, and directly, it sealed the cases lying under the hut, ensuring the bottles stayed in a stable, if frozen, environment. Second, and indirectly, the ice that lay under Cape Royds' rocky landscape deterred the Terra Nova expedition from making its base here. Scott's 1910–14 British Antarctic Expedition was larger all round. Its hut had twice the floor area of Shackleton's, and Scott's shore party was more than half as big again with 16 officers and nine seamen. Had the Terra Nova hut been built at Cape Royds, it is likely Scott's party would have made greater use of the Nimrod expedition's provisions, even perhaps to the extent of extinguishing its stocks of liquor, cigarettes and cigars.

In January 2007, the Antarctic Heritage Trust restoration team dug deeper under the hut to try to clear the ice and with it clear up a mystery. Was there any whisky in the whisky cases? Two men set out to answer that question: AHT team leader Al Fastier, a New Zealand

The Nimrod Hut conservation team's camp, Cape Royds, January 2007.
NEVILLE PEAT

Shackleton's hut at Cape Royds, January 2007, when the whisky cases underneath the floor were cleared of ice. Beyond the hut is McMurdo Sound, ice-free. Part of the Cape Royds penguin colony is also visible.
NEVILLE PEAT

outdoors and remote logistics specialist with Antarctic field experience seconded from the Department of Conservation, and James Blake, an adventurous 20-year-old who had no previous polar experience. James, the son of a New Zealand yachting legend, the late Sir Peter Blake, had arrived at Scott Base on Christmas Eve for a six-week assignment at Cape Royds and turned 20 on New Year's Eve. He was the first 'Antarctic youth ambassador' for a trust set up in his father's name.

Tall and energetic, Blake arrived hungry for work. Donning cold-weather overalls, heavy-duty gloves and knee guards at Cape Royds, he was shown by Al Fastier how to excavate under the eastern wall, the stables area. I met him at the Nimrod Hut about a week after he started. Already he seemed to be a practised hand. He showed me some of the tinned matches he had recovered. Nearby were a couple of restored dog kennels, looking less beaten about than when I photographed them in the late 1970s, although the bleached and weathered wood was the same grey colour. Lying on a bale of fodder was a relic of the party times at the Nimrod Hut — the metal bung of a barrel of beer, bearing the inscription 'J. Speight & Co. Dunedin'. It was located during the 1977–78 summer season by hut caretakers David Harrowfield and Chris Buckley. Some staves and barrel hoops were also identified.

Passing through with a helicopter bringing supplies in early January 2007, I had no idea about the ice-encased whisky crates under the hut, nor about the objects already recovered from the crawl space — an axe, darkroom supplies, panes of glass and linseed oil cans still filled with oil. Through January, Al Fastier and James Blake chiselled and chipped away at the ice around the cases. They had to squeeze under the floor beyond Wild's storeroom, where it was sunless and always bitterly cold. To melt ice that

James Blake under Shackleton's hut with one of the cases of whisky and the tubes conveying heat into the crawl space.
MARK ORAMS

Weathered timber cladding, the Nimrod Hut, December 1977.
DAVID HARROWFIELD

The bung of a Speight's beer barrel, found at Cape Royds in 1977.
NEVILLE PEAT

could not be reached by hand tools, heat was pumped into the crawl space. Around their work area the wooden piles supporting the hut appeared sound despite some mould adhering to them. A reciprocating drill was their first-choice tool for ice removal, but it proved too rough and bludgeoning a method as they cleared ice from around the cases. For the close work chisels, stiff brushes and other hand tools were employed. After days of hard labour the nearest case's labelling was fully revealed — 'Mackinlay's Rare Old Highland Malt Whisky'. The words were wrapped around the head of a handsome red deer stag, antlers standing proud.

In the process of removing the ice around the first case they released something else: the fetching scent — no mistaking it — of whisky. Whether in this crate or another, at some time in the past a bottle or bottles had broken. Hopefully there were some intact ones left. The case newly liberated appeared to be full of bottles wrapped in straw, frozen solid. Part of its wooden lid had been removed, maybe jemmied. From the conservators, led by Robert Clendon, came instructions to leave the case in situ and make no attempt to de-ice it. But that did not calm speculation among the rest of the team about how good it would be to sample a bottle.

During the ice removal, three more cases were revealed, making five in all — two were of Australian brandy from the Hunter Valley, the other two carried the Mackinlay whisky label on the long sides and 'British Antarctic Expedition 1907' on one end. So there were three whisky cases. Media reporting of this discovery was initially low-key, probably because no one could confirm how many bottles were intact and filled with the original spirit and not, as one member of the team idly thought, filled with urine as a joke.

Anticipating melt-water streams running under the hut, the 2007 team had built a waterproof dam around it. But the following summer the dam failed, sending water under the building that formed ice about 20 cm thick. It was a setback.

In the summer of 2008–09, the fate of the whisky crates was again playing on the minds of the conservators and preparations were made to excavate the cases to prevent any damage from melt-water incursions. Relocation of the whisky to Scott Base after Christmas was always going to involve helicopters because retreat of the sea ice precluded sledging. But helicopter schedules that summer were under so much pressure that the flight which was to have taken the whisky did not proceed.

What did proceed, however, was a discussion with the Scottish whisky company that had acquired the Mackinlay label through a series of mergers and takeovers — Whyte & Mackay, of Glasgow. The company had expressed a strong interest in obtaining samples of the whisky for chemical analysis. The samples would provide a unique insight into the fermentation, distillation and blending practices prevailing at the turn of the 20th century. They might also guide Antarctic Heritage Trust decisions on how to manage the rest of the Nimrod Hut whisky collection. In addition, Whyte & Mackay master blender Richard Paterson felt the whisky could still be drinkable and taste exactly as it did 100 years ago. If he could get his nose into a sample, he would try to replicate it. A tantalising prospect, for sure, but the New Zealand authorities — the Antarctic Heritage Trust in Christchurch and Ministry of Foreign Affairs and Trade (MFAT) in Wellington — needed to work through the repatriation of the whisky in compliance with Antarctic Treaty strictures. Nothing of heritage value was meant to leave Antarctica without a permit. MFAT officials were keen not to rock the treaty boat. Besides the international bureaucratic hurdles there were logistical and conservation challenges. These were the domain of AHT executive director Nigel Watson, who had a legal background as well as over a decade of experience in Antarctic heritage issues.

Multi-party discussions bubbled on. They were stirred further by the Mackinlay family. Descendants of the Mackinlays who produced the whisky wanted a bottle or two at least to return to the homeland. The heritage value was immense. Donald Mackinlay, a direct descendant of the original Charles Mackinlay, and Donald's younger brother, Ian, were especially keen, as was their New Zealand-based cousin, Charles Mackinlay Usher, of Kaiapoi — all of them fifth-generation Mackinlays. Donald Mackinlay, a renowned blender, had been with the old firm for over 40 years, retiring in 1990. No question, the Mackinlays wanted to find out if the 100-year-old whisky would pass muster.

Through the winter of 2010, a pathway for the whisky was clarified. In October, the Antarctic Heritage Trust applied for a permit from the New Zealand Minister of Foreign Affairs, under the Antarctica (Environmental Protection) Act 1994, to allow three Mackinlay bottles from Cape Royds to be transported to Scotland for 'scientific anaylsis' on the condition that the bottles were subsequently returned to Antarctica. The permit was granted for the purposes of restoration, conservation and/or protection in accordance with the Cape Royds area's management plan. Of utmost importance was mitigating any risk associated with the removal, storage, transport and return of the whisky.

Earlier, in November 2009, the discovery of crates of century-old whisky under the Shackleton hut had suddenly become news again. The London *Daily Mail* Foreign Service reported that the

Antarctic Heritage Trust team would aim to recover the whisky in January 2010. AHT field team expedition leader Al Fastier, predicting that most of the whisky would remain on Ross Island, made this comment: 'It's better to imagine it than taste it — that way it keeps its mystery.'

As 2009 rolled into 2010, Fastier and the lead summer conservator that season, Lucy Skinner, worked long hours to extract the five cases from underneath the hut. They took some moving. Each weighed, in its frozen state, around 40 kilograms. Two Mackinlay cases and two of brandy from the Hunter Valley Distillery Company's Allandale plant were stored in Mawson's Lab for the time being, where they would remain frozen. The fifth case, which had been uncovered in 2007, the one with the jemmied lid, was placed in a specially built and insulated wooden box with sturdy handles. Fastier reported to his Christchurch office that he could hear liquid sloshing inside the ice-filled whisky case.

The recovery job, undertaken with mounting excitement on Ross Island, took just over a month. On 5 February 2010, the Antarctic Heritage Trust, through a media release, announced the momentous recovery after informing Whyte & Mackay in Scotland. The trust said ice had damaged some of the cases and penetrated them and this would complicate inspection of the contents. A New Zealand television news team was on hand to record for world media the dispatch to Christchurch of the case in its insulated box. Conservators Lucy Skinner and Fran Clarke were its escorts on the flight from McMurdo Sound to Christchurch in a United States Air Force C-17 Globemaster, one of the cavernous, droopy-winged, four-engined jet aircraft that routinely fly to the Ice from Christchurch in support of the United States Antarctic Program. The box was kept in a chiller compartment at the rear of the plane. At Christchurch

International Airport, the box, like any first-class luggage, was put through an x-ray. Now, for the first time, the conservators could see intact bottles inside it. For AHT Artefacts Programme Manager Lizzie Meek it was something of a eureka moment: 'We could clearly see liquid inside some of them. Fantastic.'

Newspapers, radio stations and television channels generated a news storm as the box arrived in Christchurch, and magazine writers clamoured for interviews about the whisky and its history on the Ice. Although AHT announcements told of the 'bonus' of discovering two cases of brandy under Shackleton's hut, the media took about as much notice as if the 'unexpected find' of brandy had been lime juice.

Meanwhile, Whyte & Mackay's Richard Paterson, one of Scotland's most respected whisky 'noses', chimed in with more comments. In a story in *The Guardian*, he summed up the discovery simply and dramatically as 'a gift from the heavens' for whisky lovers. Dapper, debonair and articulate, Paterson kept talking up the opportunity to replicate the Old Highland Malt, saying it would be of 'mutual benefit'. It would allow people to 'taste a true part of history and be part of what must be the whisky story of the century'.

The original recipe for the Mackinlay Scotch from the 1890s no longer existed, so the only way of replicating it was through obtaining a sample. Paterson: 'Whiskies back then — a harder age — were all quite heavy and peaty and that was the style. We're going to extract the whisky with a syringe, and we have to make sure there's no damage whatsoever to the label or the capsule.'

The preservation message was certainly sinking in. But first, Whyte & Mackay had to get its hands on the three bottles for sampling.

From the Operation Deep Freeze base at Christchurch Airport the box was driven to Canterbury Museum. There, the whisky case inside it, still largely iced up and weighing 38.5 kilograms, was placed in a chest freezer for several months while museum staff and AHT's Lizzie Meek discussed a strategy for thawing it. No one had tackled a conservation project quite like this before.

What they came up with was a custom-built coolroom, a 2.4 metre cube with 100 millimetre-thick walls, floor and ceiling, temperature and humidity controls and a triple-glazed window. Its door resembled a refrigerator door, padlocked. It was a coolroom worthy of Fort Knox. Except for the public viewing. Buoyed by the media coverage and the demonstrated public interest, Canterbury Museum and the Antarctic Heritage Trust decided the thawing of a case of 100-year-old whisky with Shackleton's name attached to it was a publicity break not to be missed. The coolroom was set up in the museum's visitor lounge adjacent to a permanent Antarctic gallery, which featured heroic-era exhibits and a fascinating collection of Shackleton and Scott memorabilia. Members of the public were invited to drop in during opening hours and witness 'The Great Whisky Crate Thaw', and a video camera was set up to transmit pictures of the process to the world via the Internet. Let the show begin . . .

At what rate should the defrosting occur? Too fast and there could be damage to the wooden case, the packaging, capsule and labels or even the whisky itself. Moisture and its consort, mould, were potential threats. Museum conservator Sasha Stollman and her colleagues were none the wiser from searching the Internet for advice. They had to follow their experience and instincts. Whyte & Mackay recommended the whisky be kept chilled at four degrees Celsius, refrigerator temperature, consistent with

The coolroom at Canterbury Museum with the whisky crate thawing.
ANTARCTIC HERITAGE TRUST

'original preserved quality'. From minus 20 degrees, the coolroom temperature was raised very gradually — as high as eight degrees at one stage — but the temperature of the bottles themselves remained at around four degrees. The whole process took about three weeks, starting in the third week of July.

Public and online interest astonished the project's managers. YouTube live streaming attracted 108,000 hits in a matter of days, and hundreds of visitors filed into the museum to observe the silent thawing. Master blender Paterson was among the many website watchers in Scotland. The anticipation was palpable. 'It would be the highlight of my career to date,' enthused Paterson, 'to be able to analyse and replicate this liquid gold.'

AHT's Lizzie Meek was more circumspect. She made no promises on what the process could deliver. 'What does it look like, what's inside there? We don't know yet. Is there going to be anything left?' Her last comment was a reference to the apparent leakage from the case.

As the defrosting despatched the ice, an amber liquor began collecting around the case, which was mounted on blocks to avoid immersion. Allowed a close-up look at this development, Christchurch whisky retailer and connoisseur Michael Fraser-Milne, owner of the downtown store Whisky Galore, took a whiff and pronounced the liquor's bouquet 'nice floral . . . not smoky . . . a bit woody'. His heart, he admitted later, was beating quite a lot faster at being close to the thawing bottles and seeing penguin feathers. Conservator Stollman considered the melt water's properties to be the result of a combination of leaching components, including tannins from the crate timber, straw and paper wrappings, soil and scoria, together with whisky leaked from one or more bottles.

The whisky case thawing
at Canterbury Museum.

Straw wrapping on 104-year-old
bottles of Mackinlay's whisky.

On Friday, 13 August 2010 — 102 years, seven months and 13 days after the sailing of *Nimrod* from Lyttelton — the thawing was over. The conservators could now see that the labels on the bottles bore the name 'Endurance' — an unwitting tribute to the whisky itself.

Each bottle, in turn, was removed from the case complete with its straw wrapping and raffia ties and gently placed in a fabric sling made of Reemay, a strong polyester material. Each bottle had its own Reemay 'hammock', soft bedding that allowed the tissue paper and straw to dry out. The conservators noted that the bottles were of green glass with rounded shoulders and a punt in their base. Distinctively, there was a small round hole on the glass base. No maker's mark was found. Stamped on the foil capsule were the words 'Mackinlay's: Leith: Liqueur'.

In the course of the unpacking there were surprises. The first was that one bottle from the top layer was missing, although its straw packaging had held its shape to give an impression the case might contain its full complement of 12 bottles. Who had removed the bottle? Was the case sprung during the Nimrod expedition? Did Ernest Joyce, part-time penguin collector, get to work on it in the spring of 1916? He would probably have known there was a stash of whisky under the hut. Perhaps another member of Shackleton's Ross Sea Support Party on a visit to Cape Royds was responsible? Even someone from Scott's Terra Nova expedition, perhaps? Whoever and whenever, the bottle must have been taken from the case before the ice permanently sealed the rest. It is tempting to think the missing bottle ended up inside the hut, empty and with candle wax around its neck, and was whipped away by a souvenir-seeking American navyman in the summer of 1956–57. But more on that later.

The second surprise was the presence of Adelie penguin feathers amongst the bottles, blown into the crates with sprinkles of volcanic sand. For the conservators, these environmental 'extras' brought the Cape Royds setting right into their laboratory. What also stood out was the number stamped on the case — 1745. It was consistent with the typed order letter of 19 June 1907, signed by Shackleton, which requested the numbering of the 25 whisky cases, 12 brandy and six port in sequence from 1733 to 1775. Presumably the case at the Canterbury Museum was the 12th of the whisky order.

Of no surprise was the discovery that one bottle, part-filled with whisky, was leaking from a hairline crack, damaged perhaps when the case was jemmied open. It was still sealed. The remaining 10 bottles were intact, although some of the labels were disintegrating. The three bottles chosen for the journey home were judged to be the most likely to stand up to the long trip and the scheduled sampling by syringe through the capsule.

All 11 bottles were conveyed from the Great Thaw chiller — which many followers of the Shackleton whisky story regarded as the coolest coolroom in the world — into a secure storage area at Canterbury Museum, awaiting further conservation treatment, including scoria removal and consolidation of the paper wrappers, and arrangements for the repatriation of the chosen three.

Then, on 4 September, before dawn, Christchurch was shattered by an earthquake of magnitude 7.1, centred 45 kilometres west of the city at a depth of only 11 kilometres. Damage was widespread, but miraculously there were no deaths and few injuries attributable to the severe shaking. Aftershocks were incessant.[41] In individual, well-cushioned comfort deep inside Canterbury Museum, the Mackinlay whisky lay unmoved and unaffected.

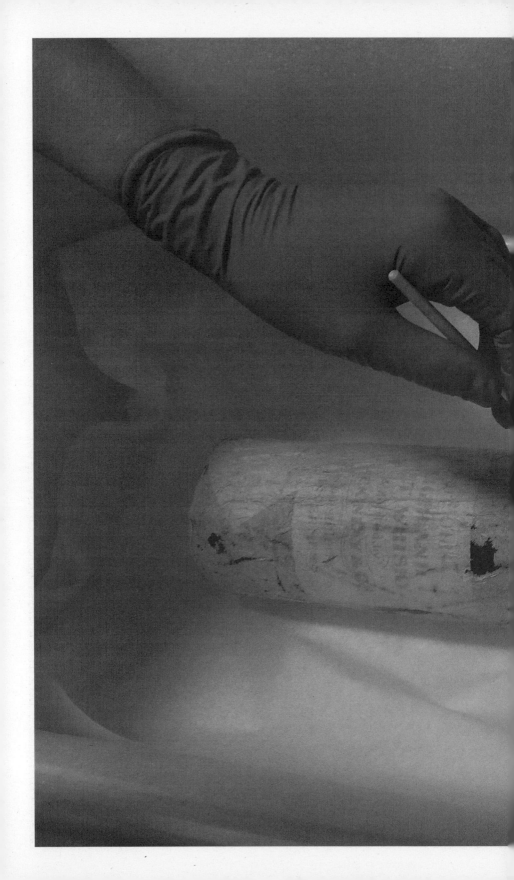

Conservation work on one of the bottles of whisky at Canterbury Museum.

20 —
PUT TO
THE NOSE

F orget the media glare, the international spotlight as it came in from the cold. Will the whisky deliver its promise? There is only one way to find out: it has to return whence it came. This time there will be no rolling and pitching through the Bay of Biscay, no rounding of Africa or jousting with the restless Southern Ocean. A hundred years on, the whisky will fly — first-class.

Richard Paterson, 'The Nose', arrives in Christchurch to formally receive and solemnly sign for the bottles, dressed in a dark suit, white shirt, red tie and red pocket handkerchief, and fully aware he is a link in whisky history. The occasion is recorded by various media, including a Talkback Thames film crew making a documentary film about the famous whisky. Adding status are Whyte & Mackay owner Vijay Mallya, Canterbury Museum director Anthony Wright, Antarctic Heritage Trust Board chairman Paul East, and the British High Commissioner, Vicki Treadell, who knows Dr Mallya from her Mumbai posting a few years earlier and who has had a hand in stimulating his interest in the polar whisky saga.

Whyte & Mackay's owner, Dr Vijay Mallya, and master blender Richard Paterson with an original full bottle and an empty one that was used as a candle-holder at the Nimrod Hut.

Two high-tech insulated containers ('chilly bins' to a New Zealander), manufactured by The Cool Icebox Company of Devon, England, are filled with ice and gel packs for the transport of the three bottles. The red bins leave Christchurch on a balmy midsummer's evening in January 2010 aboard Dr Mallya's private jet. The red-and-white Airbus 319 of the Indian billionaire has been at Christchurch for just 13 hours. After take-off, Paterson pushes back the padded easy chair and lights a celebratory cigar. Nearby, secure in a corner of the owner's cabin, a far cry from Ernest Shackleton's cabin at Cape Royds, the whisky sits in the red containers.

New Zealand officials have stipulated that the containers are not to fly by ordinary commercial aircraft (which do not allow liquids and gels exceeding 100 ml as hand-carry in the cabin) and shall not be placed in the aircraft's baggage hold.[42] They must go first-class, beside the posh leather seats. They must be in the constant care of an appropriate courier, who will handcuff himself to the bins if need be. They reach Scotland in about the time it took the Nimrod to escape the tides of the English Channel a century earlier on her long voyage south.

From a wintry Glasgow, the red chilly bins are carried north by road through the snow-laden Highlands to the Inverness area, still in the custodial care of Richard Paterson and still sporting handcuffs to prove it. They have an appointment with Whyte & Mackay's white-coated chemists, led by Dr James Pryde, at the company's laboratory at Invergordon, about 40 kilometres north of Inverness on Cromarty Firth.

The big day has arrived. The moment of truth.

Whyte & Mackay have promised not to uncork any of the bottles. A glass syringe with a surgical needle is the designated extraction tool. The cork is expected to 'heal up' once the needle is removed and the whisky is extracted, so long as it has kept its integrity. It will swell to fill the tiny void — the magic of cork. So in a sterile, well-lit stainless steel cabinet under glass, gloved hands introduce the 150 millimetre (six-inch) syringe needle into the first bottle, penetrating the protective capsule and cork. Then a fine biopsy needle is inserted alongside the sampling needle to allow air into the bottle as the whisky is withdrawn. With the sampling needle attached to a 100 millilitre glass syringe, Dr Pryde begins drawing off the whisky. It seeps into the syringe. Paterson is spellbound — his first proper look at Shackleton's whisky. For the whisky itself, kept so long in this bottle inside a case inside ice, it is a coming-out.

Samples of varying size are extracted from the three 700 millilitre bottles, with the first bottle giving up 600 millilitres. The process is repeated for all three bottles in the coming days. Altogether about 1000 millilitres is extracted. The sampled whisky is aliquoted into numbered vials for the chemical testing at the Invergordon laboratory, the Scotch Whisky Research Institute in Edinburgh and several other external laboratories. So far, so good. The colour is straw gold, shimmering under the laboratory lights. It looks the part. There is no sign of suspended sediment that would indicate deterioration. What about the nose and taste?

A sample of the whisky is removed to the nosing room where Paterson begins the sensory analysis. He rolls it around in the belly of his elegant tulip-shaped tasting glass, a practised roll to give it the aroma-releasing stimulation of fresh air while ensuring none escapes. He swirls the golden liquid and lets it warm more, knowing more elements will be released with the warming. Another nose, then another swirl and a further nosing. Now the urbane master blender, whose nose has been insured in the past with Lloyd's of London for US$2.6 million, breaks into a smile, a smile that has 'Yes!' written all over it. He has been practising his highly specialised profession for more than 40 years but never before has he had an experience like this. He turns to the chief chemist and slowly, in jerky phrases while continuing to sniff, he makes his pronouncement on the whisky: 'So, the initial reaction, is very good . . . a light style . . . lovely ripe gooseberries and that apple, pear — it's got very fresh fruit. It's very delicate, it's got floral notes, and this is suggesting an element of Speyside style . . . crushed almonds are just a whisper towards the end, and there's ripe pineapple . . . American white oak gives it charm, gives it sensuality.' The American oak comment is perceptive; the analysis to identify the kind of barrels the whisky matured in has yet to happen.

The cameras are rolling but you sense he is not merely playing to an audience when he declares: 'To my mind this is the most exciting part of my life. Seeing a whisky from the 19th century that's been preserved for well over a hundred years — that's an honour, that's a privilege. Excellent! Bloody marvellous. Sir Ernest Shackleton, I salute you!'

The Nose has tasted and assessed Shackleton's whisky. It seems like a blessing. Now for the scientific analysis.

21 —
A GIFT FROM
THE HEAVENS

Three hundred millilitres is a small bottle of cream. Or 10 drams at 30 millilitre measure. Or just one millilitre for every bottle Shackleton shipped south. Whichever way you look at it, the average amount of whisky extracted by syringe from each of the three bottles at Whyte & Mackay's Invergordon laboratory does not amount to very much. For rigorous scientific analysis in the 21st century, however, using state-of-the-art technology, you do not need a lot.

The samples, described by Richard Paterson as 'a gift from the heavens', were divided into glass bottles and subsequently much smaller vials, then put through a testing regime of forensic intensity. A 'fingerprint' was what the chemists sought, the Mackinlay whisky's signature. The chemical uniqueness of each whisky can be identified and measured through methods such as gas chromatography, olfactometry and mass spectrometry. The Scotch Whisky Research Institute in Edinburgh undertook much of this work, along with Edinburgh Scientific Services and Campden BRI in Gloucestershire. Levels of ethyl esters, sugars, acidity, phenols, anions, cations and metals were measured. Microbiological analysis indicated no contamination. Clearly, cork and capsule had sealed the whisky well. Radiocarbon dating indicated that it was as old as its history suggested.

As for alcohol content, the bottle itself did not specify the percentage by volume — regulations did not require distilleries to record the alcohol by volume (ABV) until 1907 (or the age of the whisky), by which time the Mackinlay whisky was on its way to the Ice — but something in the order of 40 per cent was a fair guess. The sample delivered a surprisingly high result — 47.19 per cent.

The higher the alcohol content, the lower the freezing point of whisky. The Mackinlay whisky's freezing point was measured as minus 34.3 degrees Celsius, with a margin of error of 1.5 degrees. At minus 34 degrees it turned to slush and only became solid well below minus 40 degrees. Under the Cape Royds hut and inside the straw packaging the bottles would have been protected from extreme cold and probably did not freeze.

Whisky in 'new-make' form distilled from pot stills is as clear as gin or vodka but has more complexity due to its unique complement of higher alcohols. The colour is acquired from the toasted wooden casks in which the spirit is left to age — a minimum of three years in the case of Scotch. From the levels of fructose and glucose and the compounds formed from the breakdown of lignins in the cask wood during maturation, the chemists concluded that the Mackinlay whisky had matured in oak casks for five to 10 years, but more likely the latter. The chemical analysis suggested the barrels were of American oak rather than European oak — more specifically, 'first fill' American oak sherry or wine casks, imported from the United States in the 19th century. The aromas associated with sherry cask maturation include woody, sweet, dried fruit and spice, and, independently, these scents were picked out by a panel of 15 expert 'noses' at the Scotch Whisky Research Institute.

This panel of researchers, nosing the whisky mixed with water at a standard 1:2 dilution, was guided by their institute's flavour wheel. The researchers found similarity in all three samples — 'a balance of peaty, mature woody, sweet, dried fruit and spicy aromas'. There were also 'floral', 'fresh fruit' and 'green grass' hints. The 'peaty' component did not dominate. If it were a 21st-century whisky, it would be characterised as 'lightly peated'. As for colour, prune juice was sometimes added by whisky makers around the turn of the 19th century, but the scientists concluded that, given the quality of the barrel wood available at the time, the addition of a colouring agent was probably not necessary.

Dr James Pryde and his colleagues went to some lengths to analysis the peat component. During kilning, the burning of peat imparts to the malted barley distinct flavours that pass into the spirit on distillation. As they reported in a scientific paper published by the *Journal of the Institute of Brewing* in 2011, they were able to compare the peat-derived phenol chemistry of the Mackinlay whisky with other malt whiskies whose peat origins were known. What they concluded was that the phenolic profile of the Mackinlay whisky was very similar to whisky currently produced using Orkney peat, confirming the historical records that peat was delivered to the Inverness distillery from the Isle of Eday.

They also found that the water used in the production was of good quality — Loch Ness and River Ness water drawn from the Caledonian Canal at Inverness. No contaminants turned up in the testing, and heavy metal analysis showed no abnormally high values.

The absence of haze or cloudiness in the whisky Shackleton

ordered was mildly surprising to the chemists, given its long exposure to low temperatures. In malt whisky, ethyl esters form long chains that can precipitate and cause cloudiness, and today many whiskies are polished by chill filtration to remove the long ester chains. The Mackinlay whisky, though, was bright and clear and seemingly destined for a long shelf life. Another conclusion: the whisky recovered from the Ice was a malt whisky, made up of malt distillations of varying age, rather than one blended with grain whisky.

As Dr Pryde told me in his office at Whyte & Mackay's huge Invergordon whisky production plant: 'There's no sign of grain whisky in it. I believe there was something special going on at Glen Mhor to produce such a whisky — from the production of malted barley and fermentation chemical profiles that are recognisably modern to a gentle firing up of the stills and their careful management during distillation, right through to the use of top-quality American white oak casks. Somehow they got everything right. The fact the spirit stayed intact and was drinkable after a hundred years just blew me away.'

Dr Pryde is telling me all this on a cool, wet Friday afternoon in Invergordon, when he had planned to be off work and at home with his young family. But he is clearly captivated by the Mackinlay whisky story, and continues: 'The high alcoholic content, 47 per cent by volume, has to have been a deliberate ploy to keep the longer-chain ethyl esters in solution and avoid haze formation at low temperatures. The cork, too, is an exceptional aspect. Despite its being in contact with the whisky for over 100 years there was no sign of any taint. We recently analysed it by electron microscopy. Found no sign of deterioration in the cork structure or ingress of micro-organisms.'

Whisky ages in a barrel, not the bottle. Contact with the cork can affect the contents, but in the case of the Mackinlay whisky Shackleton shipped south, which was packed lying down and stayed that way for over 100 years, the contents came through intact, at least in the three sample bottles. The amber brilliance of the sampled whisky had a clarity that amazed the scientists. It also challenged the notion that 19th-century Scotch whiskies were invariably dark, robust and peated, to the point of being described in modern times as 'harsh'.

Until now, no one had been given the opportunity to put a Scotch malt whisky over 100 years of age through the hoops of modern chemical and organoleptic testing (that is, analysing it through the human senses). James Pryde and his colleagues came to the conclusion: 'Charles Mackinlay & Co. Distillers were producing a malt whisky with an altogether more subtle character at their Glen Mhor Distillery near Inverness.' If ever there was a message in a bottle, this was it. It appears the directors of the Mackinlay company, eyeing up the United States market in the 1890s, decided to produce a lightly peated, floral style of whisky more appealing to Americans, and Shackleton ordered part of the production.

The scientists had unlocked the chemical fingerprint of a whisky from the Edwardian era and gained a picture of how it was manufactured and blended, something never before recorded for a whisky of such age and known provenance, let alone one that had been kept near-frozen for the bulk of its life. In the whisky world this was an outcome of major historical importance. They were clearly impressed by how well preserved it was — 'pristine' is how they described it — thanks largely to the skill of its manufacturers, a high alcoholic strength and reliable freezer storage. Of all the beverages and foodstuffs taken south aboard *Nimrod*, the Mackinlay whisky was arguably the only item uncontaminated. The quest to match it could proceed.

Richard Paterson knew he had a mission on his hands unlike anything in his long experience. Born into a Glasgow family steeped in whisky, the third generation to be involved in its manufacture, he regarded whiskies as time capsules filled with hidden messages, and his passion for them spilled into the Internet world through his blog site and on YouTube. He wrote:

> *I've spent long hours dissecting every part of the dram, working out thousands of permutations to try and recreate a long-ago whisky . . . How does it taste? Sheer heaven. Many people expected a really harsh or peaty whisky, thinking that in those ages it would be a rough dram, needing dilution. It's quite the opposite and that starts with the colour — a light honey and straw gold, which shimmers as you hold it up to the light. The nose is soft, elegant and refined with delicate aromas of crushed apple, pear and fresh pineapple. It has a whisper of marmalade, cinnamon and a tease of smoke, ginger and muscovado sugar . . . It has whispers of gentle bonfire smoke, slowly giving way to spicy rich toffee, treacle and pecan nuts.*

There was an underlying challenge: the match had to have impact on the palate consistent with an ABV level of around 47 per cent. It would pack a punch in addition to its heritage kick — a new but old label among the world's 2500 whisky brands. His mission was, virtually, to turn back time and recreate a near-priceless Scotch, knowing that the original, locked up in Antarctica, would never reach the market.

Paterson already knew he would need inputs from the Highlands and from Speyside, too. First stop: whisky from the old distillery of Glen Mhor (Great Glen) at Inverness, the birthplace of Shackleton's whisky. The distillery had closed in 1983 and was demolished in 1986 to make way for a retail complex. Its aged whiskies lived on, although supplies were limited. The allied distillery of Dalmore, close by, also provided malt as the base of the recreation. Floral flavours came from Speyside malts such as Longmorn, Benriach, Glenfarclas, Mannochmore, Tamnavulin and Glen Rothes. Among the Highlands malts adding to the marriage and the complexity were Balblair and Pulteney. To complete the puzzle, a hint of aged Jura was introduced.

After four months of searching out, sniffing, tasting and mixing mature malt whiskies, Paterson was satisfied he had a blend to match the replica. It was a marriage of 25 whiskies, aged eight to 30 years, with the oldest portion from Glen Mhor. He had waited five years for the sample bottles to reach Scotland; another three or four months was surely worth investing to reveal the Mackinlay whisky's heritage and get the recipe right for the replica.

Richard Paterson nosing a Scotch in his sample room in Glasgow, where he re-created Shackleton's whisky.
NEVILLE PEAT

22 —
TO MARKET

Malt whisky, according to lovers of it, is the world's No. 1 spirit. Scotch is exported to 210 countries, and across Scotland there can be as many as 20 million casks (called, in descending order of size, butts, hogsheads and barrels) filled with maturing Scotch. With a heritage harking back five centuries to when a friar monk wrote a note about a distillation in Fife in 1498, Scotch comes in various forms. Barley is the traditional basis, and from it, through the processes of malting, kilning, mashing, fermenting, distilling and maturing, a distillery will produce a batch — a single malt. The term referred in Shackleton's day, as now, to barley-based production from a single distillery.In contrast, and more commonly, there is the other category — blended whisky, which is a marriage of various batches of single malt from more than one distillery to suit a range of market tastes. Grains like wheat, rye and corn are the basis of grain whisky, the other major whisky category, which is spelt with an 'e' — whiskey — as in the United States and Ireland. Grain whiskies, too, can be blended.

Scotch whisky, always spelt without the 'e', hails from Scotland and nowhere else. It has been defined in law through the years, most recently by the Scotch Whisky Regulations 2009. It must be produced from malted barley and involve mashing and fermenting at the same distillery and maturing in 700-litre (or smaller) oak casks for at least three years. The only permitted additive in the maturing phase is caramel colouring. An alcoholic strength of at least 40 per cent is required.

Shackleton ordered Scotch. He knew something about whisky, in the opinion of Scots-born whisky retailer Michael Fraser-Milne, owner of the retail store Whisky Galore in Christchurch. 'His order displayed some knowledge all right,' says Fraser-Milne. 'He knew the value of ageing — he specified a 10-year-old line of whisky, M.L. brand — and he must been assured that Mackinlay and Co. were reputable distillers. He'd no doubt know they were suppliers to the Houses of Parliament in London.' The initials M.L. stood for 'Malt Liqueur' in those days, but, because liqueur smacks of sweetness and added sugar — anathema to whisky production — the term was abandoned and 'M.L.' gained another meaning: 'Malt Legacy'.

Fraser-Milne is the son of a whisky retailer who set up the Whisky Galore store in Banffshire, Scotland, in 1946. Since emigrating to New Zealand, he has been honoured with an international Keeper of the Quaich award (2008) for his expertise in whisky. He is of the view that Shackleton's whisky was a single malt and that the words 'Blended and Bottled by' on the label did not mean the contents were a blend of various productions from Glen Mhor and other distilleries. The Shackleton whisky could well have been a blend from various casks of aged single malt at the Glen Mhor distillery.

Through the northern spring of 2011, Richard Paterson and his marketing colleagues at Whyte & Mackay set about replicating the 1907 Mackinlay whisky — inside and out. Paterson worked on the whisky's recreation, using all the skills he had acquired in his 36 years as Whyte & Mackay's chief blender. It was all about 'balance', especially balancing 'peatiness' with the inputs from the American oak sherry barrels. Getting the peat levels right was the most difficult aspect of creating a replica. Paterson drew on whiskies between eight and 30 years of age to create his replica, whereas the original is thought to have been put together from distillations six to 12 years of age, with the older batches prevailing. The replica formulation was done in Glasgow — there are around 1000 whiskies on hand in Paterson's sample room — and the 1907 Mackinlay replica was assembled from its numerous component parts in Invergordon. The result: something greater than the sum of the parts.

The marketers, meanwhile, went to work on reproducing the labelling and packaging. They engaged graphic designers to perfectly match the words and typography of the original label, including the erroneous reference to the 'Ship *Endurance*'. Finer and more detailed work went into the capsule, its design, reproduction and labelling. Artwork for the Mackinlay logo, a red deer stag, and the associated hand-lettering are difficult to tell apart from the original. Each bottle would have its own wooden box — similar in colour to the Mackinlay wooden crate but not the same size and shape, of course — with the logo stamped on the side and the stencilled words 'British Antarctic Expedition 1907' on one end and the red initials 'M.L.' on the other. The bottles themselves were a special challenge. On the manufacturing line, 'quality controls' had to be switched off to allow a bottle with imperfections to be produced.

Inside the box, the replica bottle with its replica whisky would be swathed in crisp and curly wood shavings for a smooth ride. Creative wordsmiths came up with a title, 'The Enduring Spirit', and the story of the Mackinlay company, the expedition and the whisky remake was told in an accompanying 24-page booklet, printed on textured paper with its standout stitch binding of red thread redolent of the *Aurora Australis* expedition book produced at Cape Royds in the winter of 1907.

In many countries modern regulations governing alcohol sales and promotion require labels to state the alcoholic strength, but in recognition of the heritage nature of the Mackinlay recreation, British authorities granted Whyte & Mackay a dispensation.

The whole kit and caboodle went on sale in the United Kingdom in the autumn of 2011 for £100. Five pounds sterling per bottle was earmarked for donation to the Antarctic Heritage Trust in Christchurch in support of its heritage work on Ross Island. The 50,000 bottles in the first run would benefit the trust by about NZ$500,000. In New Zealand, AHT executive director Nigel Watson was 'delighted Whyte & Mackay recognised the hard work and value of the trust's conservation mission in Antarctica'.

The United States launch, in November 2011, was a glittering occasion. The venue was The Explorers Club in Manhattan, New York, founded in 1904, when Shackleton was thinking of how to get back to Antarctica. Many of those attending the launch had seen the National Geographic Channel screening a week earlier of *Expedition Whisky*, an hour-long documentary about the Nimrod expedition and the 2011 remake.

AHT board chairman Paul East flew over for the event, telling the crowd that for a visitor going into the huts of Shackleton and Scott 'it feels like everyone just left yesterday'. Richard Paterson, introducing the new Mackinlay and its history and always ready

A bottle of the Mackinlay replica whisky resting in wood shavings in its wooden box packaging. In terms of the labelling, the bottle is difficult to tell apart from the original.
WHYTE & MACKAY

to spread advice on how to drink whisky, said: 'It's been under the ice for 103 years but if you put ice in it tonight, I'll kill you!'

American reviewers gave the resurrected Mackinlay a decent tick. 'A meticulous modern recreation,' said one reviewer. 'Easy and untamed at the same time,' commented the Scotch Hobbyist blog, adding that the packaging was 'really cool'. From another American interviewer: 'An elegant flavorful whiskey [sic] that's a great conversation piece.'

In Britain, the ultimate accolade was delivered by renowned whisky writer, educator and broadcaster Dave Broom, of Hove, who was invited by Whyte & Mackay to taste both the original Mackinlay and the replica. Besides Richard Paterson, Broom was the only independent whisky connoisseur to taste the century-old one and its brand-new match, side by side. With 20 years of critiquing whisky behind him, Broom nosed and sampled both. Then the author of *The World Atlas of Whisky*, published in 2010, and the contributing editor for *Whisky* magazine, sat down and wrote this summary assessment:

> *The Shackleton whisky is not what I expected at all, perhaps not what anyone would have expected. It's so light, so fresh, so delicate and still in one piece — it's a gorgeous whisky. It proves that even way back then so much care, attention and thought went into whisky-making. I think the replication is absolutely bang on ... it's a very tricky whisky to replicate because you have this delicacy, subtlety and the smoke just coming through. The same sweetness, fragrance and spice and the subtle smoke are all there in the replica. I'm blown away by the experience.*

Broom said later he felt 'strangely nervy' tasting the original, not to mention humble. 'As well as being academically fascinating to try a whisky that old and one which had been preserved in such a bizarre way, it was emotionally powerful because of the connection with Shackleton. This was exactly what had touched their lips in the Antarctic.' Broom tasted only a small amount, using standard practice — 'nosed, sipped, allowed it to warm a little and after doing the same with the replica, added just a drop of water to both'.[43]

Among the first to taste the recreation was Sir Ernest's granddaughter, Hon. Alexandra Shackleton, who lives in London. Not being a whisky drinker, she had Whyte & Mackay's Richard Paterson available to counsel her on how to approach it. Her verdict: 'Amazing!' Had she been offered a taste of the original? 'Oh, no. I wasn't even allowed to touch a bottle.' To Alexandra it seemed a case of 'extreme preciousness'. She felt her grandfather would have been 'proud and mildly amused' by the appearance of a replica whisky with his name attached to it.

In Scotland, Mackinlay descendants also heaped praise on the remake. Donald Mackinlay, a blender with the company for decades till his retirement in 1990, dubbed the replica 'a very good job', especially given that the distillations that went into the 1907 product were long gone and that Richard Paterson had only modern whiskies to work with. 'What astonished everybody, though,' says Donald Mackinlay, 'was the quality of the original. Given the reliance on wooden vessels a hundred years ago wild yeasts could have spoilt the original. Incredible, too, that it wasn't cloudy after such a long time in cold storage — like the cloudiness that affects olive oil subjected to cold temperatures. That surprised everybody. Then there is the question of style. People thought it wouldn't have anything like the finesse of modern whisky — that it would be robust and heavy.'

In New Zealand, Christchurch was a focal point for the replica's launch — the home of Antarctic Heritage Trust, Antarctica New Zealand and the Whisky Galore store. Separated from Christchurch by the Port Hills, Lyttelton had been badly hit by the two big earthquakes over magnitude six, especially the shallow February 2011 rupture. The town that had farewelled *Nimrod* had been on its knees, with wharves wrecked and the Victorian Timeball Station overlooking the port, which operated in Shackleton's day, a demolition job. But Lyttelton and Christchurch at large were striving valiantly now to restore a semblance of order and stability. The recreation of an old tipple — history repeating — was the kind of lift Christchurch deserved.

New Zealand tastings were staged in Auckland and Wellington as well as in Christchurch, weeks ahead of the United States launch. In association with the Antarctic Heritage Trust, Michael Fraser-Milne's Whisky Galore business presented a whisky evening to remember — four of them. Two were held in Auckland. With a stirring entrepreneurial turn of phrase, Fraser-Milne was billed as 'the first expert anywhere in the world to inspect and smell the original whisky' on the strength of his having nosed the amber liquor seeping from the thawing case at Canterbury Museum. Articulate and knowledgeable, with a background in heritage tour guiding in Scotland, he had been the media's 'go-to man' as the case and bottles of whisky had emerged from the ice.

All four 'Enduring Spirit' tastings were booked out. Sixty whisky lovers attended each of the events. Five whiskies were offered for tasting — the replica and four of its components: Glen Mhor 1982 (a very rare whisky), Dalmore 12-year-old, Jura

10-year-old and Glenfarclas 10-year-old. The Wellington tasting was at Parliament Buildings, with the Minister of Science, Wayne Mapp, hosting. The honoured guest at the Christchurch function had a *Nimrod* connection — Mary Boyle, a daughter of crew member Felix Rooney, whose diary is in Canterbury Museum.

Fraser-Milne summed up his thoughts on the remake: 'Pretty classy. Good character and good feel in the mouth.' He used the term 'foosty' to describe a musty, old-warehouse aroma. 'What amazes me about the whole project is this: if Mackinlay's had made a whisky that was less than 40 per cent alcohol, the remnants in Antarctica would have been degraded and cloudy after all this time. End of story. Nothing worth recreating.'

Whisky Galore lost 60 per cent of its stocks in the devastating and deadly earthquake of February 2011, but by the end of the year Fraser-Milne was back in business in new premises and cheering for the Mackinlay replica; he had sold 60 cases, twice as many as Shackleton's order. 'It was phenomenal. I've never experienced anything like it. The phone calls and emails just kept coming. We've had people buying the Mackinlay whisky without even knowing what whisky tasted like.'

Dave Broom had more than one tasting of the replica and continued to praise it for its faithfulness to the flavours of the original. At the same time he was philosophical: 'It can never be the same. We cannot go back. Whisky is made in a different way these days, just as Antarctic exploration has changed. We could recreate Shackleton's expedition but we'd do it with GPS and backup crews. We could create the flavours of his whisky, but it would always be a homage and not identical. And that is how it should be.'

23 —
BACK TO THE ICE

The case of Mackinlay's Rare Old Highland Malt Whisky that was loaded in London in 1907, carried to New Zealand and Ross Island aboard *Nimrod*, returned to New Zealand by the United States Air Force a century later, and three bottles of it repatriated to Scotland by private jet . . . that much-travelled whisky was destined to make a final journey back to the old Shackleton hut and headquarters in Antarctica by the end of the summer of 2012–13.

Whyte & Mackay were given extensions of time by the New Zealand authorities and planned to fly the three part-emptied bottles back to Christchurch, where they would be reunited with the other eight bottles and its famous case. In 2013, the case would face a second trip from New Zealand to McMurdo Sound — by air this time. On Ross Island it would end up in a secure, permanent resting place in accordance with Antarctic Treaty rules about the protection of heritage objects. The Antarctic Heritage Trust was exploring ways and means of putting some of the whisky on display at the Nimrod Hut for summer visitors to admire, providing the whisky, bottles and cases were at no risk of being interfered with or stolen. Their value is only going to increase with time.

In 2011, an Australian whisky expert reckoned a full bottle of Edwardian-era Mackinlay's might fetch US$69,000 on the open market. At that price, who could afford to drink it? Had Shackleton known that whisky grew more valuable with age, he might have been tempted to bring a case or two home to help pay for the expedition over time. But did he even know there were three cases underneath his bunk at Cape Royds?

Epilogue

S ir Ernest Shackleton, knighted for his achievements on the Nimrod expedition in December 1909, the year he returned, had nothing to say in his 1909 book *The Heart of the Antarctic* about his whisky order or how it was consumed on the expedition. In the book's list of foodstuffs and beverages there is no mention of the 25 cases of Mackinlay's Rare Old Highland Malt Whisky nor any reference to the 12 cases of whisky — 'medical comforts' — ordered for the relief expedition at the end of 1908. Over four pages of the expedition book Shackleton discusses 'the more important items of our provisions' but ignores the 43 cases of whisky, brandy and port. Mind you, the wine, champagne and liqueurs never rated a mention either. The beverages he listed are non-alcoholic, notably Lipton's tea, coffee and the omnipresent Rowntree's elect cocoa.

Regarding the festive midwinter party at Cape Royds, the authorised account of the expedition is all but silent. Did Shackleton consciously turn a blind eye to the presence of alcohol and the indulgence by some members of his shore party, or did he ignore the whisky because he considered it to be of no account in the success of his expedition?

How ironic then that the whisky should illuminate his name and his hut a century year later. As a result of the discovery, thawing and replication of his whisky, 'Shackleton' and 'whisky' are now closely associated in the minds of millions of people across the United Kingdom, the United States, New Zealand, Australia and beyond.

There were collateral effects. The whisky saga was a huge public relations boost for the Antarctic Heritage Trust in New Zealand — a 'fantastic story' is how executive director Nigel Watson described it. Relying on donations to carry out an extensive programme of restoration and conservation at Antarctica's most important group of dwellings, the trust found itself thrust into the limelight in Britain and the United States, two countries with a significant interest in Shackleton and Scott.

The published and unpublished accounts of the Nimrod expedition suggest that Shackleton, if he tasted the whisky at all, consumed very little of it. Back in London, in a preface for *The Heart of the Antarctic*, he wrote of the 'faithful service and loyal cooperation' of the members of his expedition, which he described elsewhere in the book as 'a very happy little party'. Yet clearly there had been querulous times, with various members of the party expressing privately to their diaries and journals some dark and seditious thoughts about their leader and their lot in general. But no one doubted, in the end, Shackleton's leadership qualities, his even-handed approach to managing a disparate group of men, and his willingness to cut them slack when he thought it necessary, including at times of celebration.

Was he embarrassed by the quantum of whisky he had ordered, 300 bottles? He had no need to be, according to a retired Royal Navy officer, Commander Peter Lankester, of Wiltshire, who served on frigates in the Atlantic and flew navy helicopters in the 1980s. During his time as a pilot he flew over the mountains, snow and ice of subantarctic South Georgia, where Shackleton and his companions trekked in 1916 to reach the Norwegian whaling station and organise the rescue of the stranded men of his Endurance expedition. As Commander Lankester pointed out to me, the Royal Navy issued a daily tot of 50 per cent-proof rum to all sailors until 1970. A standard tot was one-eighth of a pint or 71 millilitres. 'If my calculations are correct, each man would have consumed the equivalent of three bottles of spirits per month or a case in four months. Put in this context the quantity of whisky on Shackleton's expedition does not seem excessive!'

Quite so. The Mackinlay bottles held 700 millilitres, equivalent to about 10 tots. Taken on a daily basis the traditional tot can start to add up — three bottles a month, as Commander Lankester says. The 15 men on the Nimrod expedition were based at Cape Royds or in the field for 13 months. At the rate of three bottles a month each man would have consumed 39 bottles by the time they boarded *Nimrod* for the voyage home. Multiplied by 15, that amounts to 585 bottles for the whole expedition — almost twice as much as Shackleton ordered! Of course, it was a long time between drinks for many members of the Nimrod team. Some were wary of alcohol full stop, even at party time, and alcohol and sledging were incompatible, with sledging for the most part an exercise in survival.

Yet Shackleton surely regarded the whisky as more than a 'medical comfort'. He would have valued its contribution to camaraderie during the confinement and tedium of winter as well as at times of hardship and when the cold became too intense. Commander Lankester: 'If I were Shackleton I would have done the same [taken a stock of whisky and other spirits], even if my own personal feelings were against drink. The fact that Shackleton looked at all aspects of the potential use and abuse of alcohol, and then decided to take such quantities despite huge logistical hurdles, shows his perception that the potential benefits outweighed the risks.'

After Nimrod, Shackleton led two more Antarctic expeditions — the 1914–17 Endurance bid to cross the whole continent and the Quest expedition of 1921–22, officially known as the British Oceanographic and Subantarctic Expedition, which aimed to map in detail as much of the Antarctic coastline as possible, undertake marine and earth studies and explore remote islands. But before the Quest expedition could get down to work Shackleton died, suddenly, aged 47, of a massive heart attack in the early hours of 5 January 1922, when the ship was at the Norwegian whaling port of Grytviken, South Georgia. Shackleton was buried among the whalers' graves on the island that meant so much to him. His old sledging friend and fellow explorer, Frank Wild, took over as leader of the expedition.

In modern times there have been a number of expeditions retracing the Antarctic journeys of Ernest Shackleton. In 2008–09,

The three members of the Shackleton centennial expedition that reached the South Pole carrying the 1907 expedition's compass. From left: Henry Adams, Henry Worsley and Will Gow.
HENRY WORSLEY COLLECTION

three descendants of the Nimrod explorers — Will Gow (great-nephew of Shackleton), Henry Adams (great-grandson of Jameson Boyd Adams) and the team leader, Lieutenant Colonel Henry Worsley (a relative of Frank Worsley, the *Endurance* captain) — travelled to McMurdo Sound and trekked all the way to the South Pole from Ross Island.

Going under the name of the Matrix Shackleton Centenary Expedition, they aimed to 'finish the business'. After breakdowns and hold-ups for weather on the Ross Ice Shelf and Beardmore Glacier, the trio arrived 'mentally and physically empty' at the Nimrod expedition's Farthest South, in latitude 88 degrees, on 9 January 2009, exactly 100 years after Shackleton. From there the three men stoically walked on to the Pole and completed a total distance of 920 miles (1472 kilometres), which took them 66 days. The most precious piece of equipment Worsley carried was Shackleton's compass, borrowed from the explorer's granddaughter, Alexandra. It carried the initials 'E H S' scratched into the underside of the lid. On arrival at the Pole he took it out and saw the needle spinning. It was a sensational moment. The compass, 'irrevocably part of him [Shackleton]', had finally and physically arrived at 90 degrees South. The three modern adventurers flew out from the South Pole courtesy of the United States.

Shackleton, had he reached 'the spot worth striving for' with any or all of his companions, would almost certainly not have made it back. Roald Amundsen's sledging party, relying on husky power, was the first to do the return trip without mechanical help, but even he was impressed and emotional on passing Shackleton's Farthest South, writing: 'We were farther south than any human being had been. No other moment of the whole

Hon. Alexandra Shackleton with a precious heirloom — the compass used by her grandfather on his 1908–09 Southern Journey. The compass was taken on the 2008 centennial expedition that followed in Shackleton's footsteps and carried it all the way to the South Pole.
NEVILLE PEAT

Larger than life, this sculpture of Sir Ernest Shackleton greets visitors to the Royal Geographical Society's headquarters in Kensington, London.
NEVILLE PEAT

trip affected me like this. The tears forced their way to my eyes.'

Anyone who walks and sails in the footsteps or wake of Sir Ernest Shackleton in modern times faces a Herculean challenge. The routes may look the same, and even the food and equipment may bear some resemblance, but a modern expedition has modern backups that Shackleton could not have dreamed of — global positioning systems (GPS), satellite phones, helicopters and so on. As whisky expert Dave Broom says: 'It can never be the same.' A century on, things are inevitably different and all we can do is pay homage.

At the start of the modern era of Antarctic research and exploration, the years leading up to and immediately following the International Geophysical Year of 1957–58, official and individual attitudes to heritage protection were rather more relaxed than they are today. Certain objects in the old huts on Ross Island were sitting-duck souvenirs. Some even attracted publicity. The December 1956 edition of *Harpers Wine and Spirit Gazette* ran a story headlined 'Old Antarctic Camp's Whisky', which described the discovery of an empty Mackinlay's whisky bottle inside Shackleton's hut. A group of United States Navy men led by Lieutenant Clarence Hadley, of Operation Deep Freeze, arrived at the hut by helicopter and, as he told the magazine, the whisky bottle was resting on a shelf above a bunk with the stump of a candle inserted in the neck. 'I was the first to enter. It gave me a creepy feeling. It looked exactly as if there should have been someone there still. Put it another way — it was a kind of Marie Celeste situation but on land, or rather ice. Tables, chairs, bunks with sleeping bags still in them, boots and shoes underneath the bed, seal blubber waiting to be cooked beside the stove, tins of soup and mustard, boxes of matches, whole hams hanging from the rafters . . .'

That bottle is now a prized possession of Scotland's Mackinlay family. Some time after it was removed from the Nimrod Hut, Lieutenant Hadley delivered it to the Mackinlay company office in Waterloo Place, London. His reward: a couple of cases of 12-year-old Mackinlay whisky. In 2012, retired blender Donald Mackinlay, his brother Ian and son Nial produced the bottle when we gathered for a meeting in their home valley of Calvine, near Pitlochry. The previous year the bottle had been lent to Whyte & Mackay for its marketing department to study the labelling and set up a photo shoot with a candle flame dripping creamy new wax over the aged brown wax around the bottle's neck.

Donald Mackinlay believes — and so do I — that the bottle is the famous missing one, removed by a person or persons unknown from one of the cases under the Nimrod Hut many years before the rediscovery — the case subsequently thawed at Canterbury Museum.

Visitors to the Nimrod Hut in the summer of 1956–57 also included New Zealand's legendary mountaineer and Antarctican, Sir Edmund Hillary, conqueror of Mount Everest, who was involved with the construction of New Zealand's Scott Base at Hut Point. His experience of the hut was rather different from Lieutenant Hadley's. As Sir Edmund recalled years later, it was the only time he ever had a ghostly experience. He opened the door and went through the porch: '... I distinctly saw Shackleton walking towards me and welcoming me and then it all sort of flashed away and he was gone.' Sir Edmund, who died in January 2008 aged 88, recalled the incident during the filming of a video in 2004–05 in support of fundraising for the restoration of the heroic-era huts on Ross Island.

The Nimrod Hut has been described as a time capsule — likewise the whisky, which we now know exhibits a whisper of Orcadian peat and Speyside flavour infusions.

The original 1907 order signed by Ernest Shackleton is a valued possession of the Mackinlay family. Holding it are Nial Mackinlay (left), the son of Donald Mackinlay and a sixth-generation descendant of company founder Charles Mackinlay, and his uncle, Ian Mackinlay, both of whom live at Calvine near Pitlochry.
NEVILLE PEAT

For 21st-century visitors to McMurdo Sound, Shackleton's hut is a highlight, if not the highlight, of their entire tour to the Ice. At each visit by a tour ship a procession of Zodiac inflatable craft will ferry passengers to Back Door Bay, from where they are guided to the Pony Lake area and the hallowed hut. Even on a mild day at Cape Royds they are dressed for a blizzard, cumbersome in their head-to-toe cocooning of protective gear. They are under strict instructions as to where they can walk. A management plan determines numbers — no more than 40 in the hut's area of special protection, and no more than eight inside the hut at any one time. In an average summer season, Cape Royds gets as many as 2000 visitors, who come by tour ship or by helicopter from McMurdo Station and Scott Base.

Imagine Shackleton standing at the porch entrance, surveying the scene on a tour-ship day. He is dressed in a dull old woollen jumper he has worn for months, a cigarette casually in hand. He eyes up the drifts of bright red padded jackets with mild amusement, his blue eyes reflecting the white Royal Society mountains across the sound. Now he is inviting you in for a steaming hot cup of Plasmon cocoa. He shows you his cosy cabin and bids you warm up at the glowing stove. He may even offer you a wee dram — a spirit with staying power, a lasting legacy.

Tourists from the expedition ship *Orion* enjoying a fine day at Cape Royds, January 2010.
DANIEL DAVIS/ORION EXPEDITION CRUISES

Visitors to Shackleton's hut at Cape Royds return to their expedition ship *Orion* from Back Door Bay, February 2011.
RICHARD WINSTON/ORION EXPEDITION CRUISES

Remains of a BAE crate at Cape Royds, amidst the penguin colony, January 2012.
SCOTT JENNINGS, COURTESY OF DAVID AINLEY

Shackleton's Shore Party

JAMESON BOYD ADAMS — Second-in-command, meteorologist; Royal Naval Reserve lieutenant; born 1880 Rippingale, Lincolnshire; died 1962.

BERTRAM ARMYTAGE — pony handler, general assistant; soldier and artilleryman in South African War; born 1869 Lara, Victoria; died 1910.

SIR PHILIP LEE BROCKLEHURST — assistant geologist; graduate of Eton College and Cambridge University; born 1887 near Leek, Staffordshire; died 1975.

PROFESSOR TANNATT WILLIAM EDGEWORTH DAVID — chief scientist, geologist, glaciologist; Oxford graduate and Professor of Geology at the University of Sydney; born 1858 St Fagans, Wales; died 1934.

BERNARD C. DAY — motor car engineer, electrician; mechanic with Arrol-Johnston Motor Company; born 1884 Oakham, Leicestershire; died 1934.

ERNEST EDWARD MILLS JOYCE — in charge of sledges, dogs, general stores, zoological collections; Royal Navy petty officer, South African War service and member of the National Antarctic Expedition 1901–04; born 1875 Bognor, Sussex; died 1940.

DR ALISTAIR FORBES MACKAY — assistant surgeon, assistant zoologist; Edinburgh University graduate, South African War service, Royal Navy surgeon; born 1878 Carskiey, Kintyre; died 1914.

DR ERIC STEWART MARSHALL — surgeon, cartographer, photographer; Cambridge University graduate and St Bartholomew's Hospital surgeon, rugby football captain; born 1879 Hampstead, London; died 1963.

GEORGE EDWARD MARSTON — artist; Regent Street Polytechnic graduate and art teacher; born 1882 Portsmouth; died 1940.

DOUGLAS MAWSON — physicist, geologist; graduate of the University of Sydney, lecturer in mineralogy and petrology at Adelaide University, curator South Australia Museum; born 1882 Shipley, Yorkshire; died 1958.

JAMES MURRAY — biologist, microscopic zoologist; biologist for the Scottish Lake Survey 1902–07; born Glasgow 1865; died 1914.

RAYMOND EDWARD PRIESTLEY — geologist; studied at Bristol University College; born 1886 Tewkesbury, Gloucestershire; died 1974.

WILLIAM C. ROBERTS —cook; chef in the British Merchant Navy and ashore in various places; born 1872 London.

JOHN ROBERT FRANCIS WILD — stores manager and sledge-master; 10 years with British Merchant Navy, joined Royal Navy as an able seaman in 1900, a member of the National Antarctic Expedition 1901–04; born 1873 Skelton, Yorkshire; died 1939.

Notes

1. Among Tennyson's most famous works is 'Ulysses', a dramatic monologue of heroic travel and adventure that ends with the line: 'To strive, to seek, to find, and not to yield'. These words are inscribed on a wooden cross in Antarctica, erected on the summit of Observation Hill, Ross Island, to commemorate the death of Robert Falcon Scott and his party, who reached the South Pole in the summer of 1911–12 but perished on the return journey.

2. Dulwich College claimed Shackleton was 'without doubt our most famous Old Boy' following his premature death in 1922 at South Georgia.

3. Browning, another great Victorian poet, who died in 1889, was born and home-schooled in a Christian home in South London, and, like Shackleton, did not excel at higher levels of formal learning. His poems sang and rang true to Ernest Shackleton, who quoted them at sea and throughout his life.

4. The title, *O.H.M.S. or How 1200 Soldiers went to Table Bay*, was sold by subscription. More than 2000 copies were sold.

5. Grain whiskey is made from cereals other than barley, typically wheat or maize.

6. In the 21st century the site is a retail complex comprising large stores that advertise products such as outdoor clothing, computers and hardware.

7. During the extraction of Loch Ness water for whisky making 100 years ago, no one reported disturbing Nessie, the fabled water monster. The loch is awash with myth and legend, and the stories about its resident water monster date back to the sixth century. Since 1933, however, sightings of an aquatic cryptid, a plesiosaur-like creature with a small head and humped body, have generated

a legend that persists. Sightings continue to be reported. Scientific investigations using manned and remote-controlled submersibles, sonar and acoustic equipment have failed to produce evidence that Nessie exists. Science does its best to explain, however, the natural phenomenon of seiches or rhythmic oscillations in lake level — 'mini-tides' that leave signatures on the beaches.

8. Peat deposits are formed over thousands of years from vegetable matter that has decomposed in bog and moor environments, and subsequently carbonised. The character of the deposits varies according to the type of vegetation forming them (trees, shrubs, herbs, grasses, ferns, mosses) and the chemicals in the environment. Deposits many metres thick are harvested as fuel resources, especially by people inhabiting regions too cold to support firewood forests. For centuries peat has been used in whisky making as a fuel in the malt kiln and an important flavouring agent.

9. Robert Falcon Scott, *The Voyage of the Discovery*, 2 vols, published by Macmillan and Co., London, 1905.

10. Sir Ernest (he was knighted in 1909) and Emily Shackleton's third child, Edward (Baron Shackleton from 1955), was born in July 1911 between the Nimrod and Endurance expeditions to Antarctica.

11. In fact, alcohol depresses the central nervous system, and its warming effect is illusory. Through dilation of the blood vessels the body actually loses heat.

12. The Scotch Whisky Act 1909 presented a legal definition of Scotch to protect its integrity in the marketplace and differentiate it from Irish and other imported whiskies.

13. The Gaelic spelling of 'Good Health' varies.

14. Instead of returning home in *Nimrod* after the delivery voyage, Professor David remained with the expedition for the year. On the voyage south, Shackleton decided the professor's expertise and guidance would be invaluable. It would be the most adventurous episode in David's life and he would return to Australia a hero.

15. Joseph (later Sir Joseph) Kinsey was also the New Zealand agent for Scott's Discovery expedition.

16. The 1898–1900 British Antarctic Expedition was led by Norwegian adventurer Carsten Borchgrevink in the vessel *Southern Cross*. Erecting two huts, the 10 men spent the winter of 1899 at Cape Adare, the Ross Sea's eastern portal. Although British sponsored, the expedition team was substantially Norwegian. It was the first party to winter on the Antarctic continent.

17. The one-penny universal New Zealand stamps, overprinted with the words 'King Edward VII Land', carried the symbolic female image of Zealandia, a version of Britannia.

18. A Royal Navy exploring expedition, under the command of Captain James Clark Ross, back in January 1841, had been the first to map the edge of the ice shelf, over 400 kilometres of it, and he concluded it would be as easy to sail a ship through the Cliffs of Dover as to penetrate what he described as the Victoria Barrier (later named the Great Ice Barrier) in honour of his new Queen.

19. In January 1911, a Norwegian expedition led by Roald Amundsen set up a base at the Bay of Whales, from where, later that year, the geographic South Pole was reached for the first time.

20. Mount Erebus was named by James Clark Ross in 1841 after the ship he commanded. In Greek mythology, Erebus was a part of the underworld through which the dead passed on their way to Hades. Ross named the second-highest peak on Ross Island after the second ship in his expedition, *Terror*, and the waterway between Ross Island and the Antarctic mainland was named McMurdo Bay after *Terror*'s commander, Lieutenant Archibald McMurdo. He retired as a vice-admiral.

21. Cape Royds was named after the *Discovery*'s first lieutenant, Charles Rawson Royds, the expedition meteorologist. He later became an admiral.

22. Captain Evans later received a gold watch from Shackleton inscribed: 'In remembrance of the towing of the Nimrod to the Antarctic Circle'. The watch is displayed in the Canterbury

Museum's Antarctic gallery with other relics from the British Antarctic Expedition 1907–09, including tins of food and a wheel from the Arrol-Johnston car.

23. In 1957, Jameson Adams, second-in-command, recalled for Shackleton biographer James Fisher memories of the social atmosphere in the hut during the four months of winter: '. . . I never heard an angry word spoken during the whole of that period. Everyone was absorbed in his own particular function or engaged in preparing for the great journey ahead. Coarse language of any sort was automatically eschewed, and alcohol was not available.' Presumably Adams meant by the last remark that alcohol was not available on demand but rather only at times of celebration.

24. The first winter visit to Cape Crozier to collect emperor penguin eggs was carried out in 1911 by members of Scott's Terra Nova expedition, including Apsley Cherry-Garrard, who wrote about it in his celebrated book, *The Worst Journey in the World*.

25. The aurora is a result of solar radiation electrically exciting ions in the ionosphere. On clear nights through autumn and winter there were numerous displays, sometimes reflected off the snow and ice. The only other colour came from Mount Erebus, where periodic eruptions in the lava lake caused clouds and steam at the summit to glow with shades of red.

26. In 1986, Bluntisham Books and the Paradigm Press of Alburgh, Harleston, Norfolk published a facsimile edition.

27. Arthur Young, *Travels in France* (two volumes), 1792; George Borrow, *The Bible in Spain*, 1843.

28. The same incident rated a mention in Priestley's diary as 'the first disagreeable fracas of the Expedition'. As Priestley saw it, Roberts had caused the disturbance by putting his feet up on a bin belonging to Mackay.

29. On a different angle of approach over the Ross Ice Shelf, Roald Amundsen's team used the Axel Heiberg Glacier, 300 kilometres south of the Beardmore, to reach the polar plateau and the South Pole on 14 December 1911.

30. The party carried more than one Union Jack. The Queen's silk flag was returned to England and Buckingham Palace. On exceptionally cold nights on the polar plateau Frank Wild would wrap himself up in it for warmth.

31. Because they had left their theodolite back at the tent, the position, calculated by dead reckoning, was an estimate only. Various assessments of the distance to run from the last camp, the time it took them, the conditions, and their fitness and energy levels have called into question their claim of getting inside 100 miles of the South Pole. To the end, Shackleton insisted they did do it and none of his party queried the achievement, not even Marshall, Shackleton's strongest critic.

32. The Magnetic South and North Poles are always on the move. In about 100 years, from Scott's Discovery expedition of 1903 to the end of the century, the South Magnetic Pole moved progressively through eight degrees of latitude and 18 degrees of longitude.

33. Three of the 10 men of the Imperial Trans-Antarctic Expedition's Ross Sea Party perished in the McMurdo Sound region. The first to die was the Rev. Arnold Spencer-Smith, who succumbed to scurvy on the way back from a southern sledging journey. Later, Lt Aeneas Mackintosh and Victor Hayward disappeared in a May blizzard on McMurdo Sound sea ice while trying to reach Cape Evans from Hut Point.

34. In January 1940, Richard Evelyn Byrd established the Little America III base at the Bay of Whales, his third expedition into the Ross Sea region. From here, before the United States entered World War II, he led the exploration of the Marie Byrd Land coast west of King Edward VII Land.

35. The International Geophysical Year (IGY) of 1957–58 had an Antarctic focus. Twelve nations set up 55 bases on or around Antarctica. Several thousand scientific and support staff were deployed to take the geophysical 'pulse' of Antarctica in disciplines such as seismology, geomagnetism, geology, meteorology and atmospheric physics. IGY started the monitoring, measuring, sensing and photographing that continues today.

36. Adelie penguins have also nested sporadically in the past at Cape

Barne, three kilometres south of Cape Royds. Scott's biologists recorded a handful of nests there in 1911, and in December 1988 New Zealand scientists recorded five nests. From his initial 1959–60 season at Cape Royds, Rowley Taylor published six papers in scientific journals, the main paper appearing in the British ornithological journal *Ibis* in April 1962. Euan Young also had papers published in *Ibis* as a result of his Antarctic studies.

37. A late breakout of the sea ice in the 1962–63 season caused a setback for the Adelies. It meant the penguins had to travel stressful distances on foot or tobogganing to get to open water and fishing grounds. Plenty of nests were abandoned.

38. *Forbush and the Penguins* might have been one of the first novels wholly set in the Antarctic, but a 1913 romantic novel, *The Woman Thou Gavest Me* by Hall Caine, included an account of a voyage to Antarctica and a trek to the South Pole that drew on Shackleton's *The Heart of the Antarctic* for some of the detail. *Forbush and the Penguins* was adapted for the 1971 film *Mr Forbush and the Penguins* (released in the United States in 1972 as *Cry of the Penguins*), starring John Hurt and Hayley Mills.

39. The Antarctic Heritage Trust is registered as a charitable entity and governed by a board of trustees. Its office is in the same complex as Antarctica New Zealand and Operation Deep Freeze at Christchurch International Airport. The trust, although receiving government funding for its staff and administration costs, depends on donations for its multimillion-dollar restoration projects.

40. Seventeen conservators were engaged for varying times through the four years of the Cape Royds project, through summer and winter (winter seasons from 2006). They came from New Zealand, Australia, Britain, Canada, Germany, the United States and Taiwan. They worked with wood, textiles, metal and paper, and with food and hazardous substances. Interest in the work grew as the Royds project gained international publicity, to the extent that for the start of the follow-up Cape Evans project there were 120 applicants for four positions.

41. On 22 February 2011, a second major earthquake (magnitude 6.3, just 10 kilometres south of the centre of Christchurch and 5 kilometres deep) struck during working hours, causing more than 185 deaths and destroying thousands of homes and business premises.

42. The transport of the three bottles to Scotland was approved by the New Zealand Minister of Foreign Affairs, which set conditions on their transport there and back, security measures, sampling methods and conservation measures. The permit also prohibited the sale, gifting or retention of the whisky or bottles.

43. Comments to the author in March 2012.

Glossary

FAST ICE — Permanant or semi-permanent ice that is typically attached to a shoreline or seabed. It does not move in currents and winds.

FINNESKO — A soft shoe designed for polar travel with no hard sole, made from reindeer skin with sennegrass (q.v.) lining; traditional footwear for Laplanders.

FRAZIL ICE — Slushy ice made up of needle-shaped crystals.

HOOSH — A thick soup made from protein-rich pemmican with hard biscuits mixed in. It might be flavoured by bacon, cheese, pea flour, oatmeal or sugar.

MAUJEE RATION — A compressed feed for ponies consisting of dried beef, carrots, milk, currants and sugar.

MANHAULING — Manual method of pulling a sledge (or other object) over snow and ice. The men wore a harness roped to the sledge.

PIEDMONT ICE — An ice sheet, typically in foothills, formed from one or more glaciers.

SASTRUGI — Wind-blown ridges in snow or ice.

SEA ICE — Seasonal ice formed through winter and spring.

SENNEGRASS — A footwear lining to keep the wearer's feet as dry and warm as possible in polar regions, made from the sedge *Carex vesicaria*.

References

BOOKS

Barnard, Alfred, *The Whisky Distilleries of the United Kingdom* (new edition 1989), Birlinn, Edinburgh, 1887.

Begbie, Harold, *Shackleton, A Memory*, Mills & Boon, London, 1922.

Billing, Graham, *Forbush and the Penguins*, A. H. & A. W. Reed, Wellington, 1965.

Branagan, David, *T. E. Edgeworth David: A Life: geologist, adventurer, soldier and 'knight in the old brown hat'*, National Library of Australia, Canberra, 2005.

Butler, Angie, *The Quest for Frank Wild*, Jackleberry Press, Warwick, 2011.

Cherry-Garrard, Apsley, *The Worst Journey in the World: Antarctic 1910–1913*, Picador, London, 1922.

Conly, Maurice (text by Neville Peat), *Ice on my Palette*, Whitcoulls, Christchurch, 1977.

Crane, David, *Scott of the Antarctic: A biography*, HarperCollins, London, 2005.

Fisher, Margery and James, *Shackleton*, James Barrie Books, London, 1957.

Hoflenher, Josef and Katharina, and David Harrowfield (text), *Frozen Legacy: The legacy of Scott and Shackleton*, Josef Hoflenher, Wels, Austria, 2003.

Huntford, Roland, *Shackleton*, Hodder & Stoughton, London, 1985.

Huntford, Roland (introduction), *The Shackleton Voyages: A pictorial anthology of the polar explorer and Edwardian hero*, Weidenfeld & Nicolson, London, 2002.

Jackson, Michael, *Malt Whisky Companion*, Dorling Kindersley, London, 1999.

Jackson, Michael, *Scotland and Its Whiskies*, Harcourt, London, 2001.

Joyce, Ernest, *The South Polar Trail: The log of the Imperial Trans-Antarctic Expedition*, Duckworth, London, 1929.

Mackintosh, A. L. A., et al., *Shackleton's Lieutenant: The Nimrod diary of A. L. A. Mackintosh, British Antarctic Expedition 1907–09*, Polar Publications, Auckland, 1990.

MacLean, Charles, *Scotch Whisky: A liquid history*, Cassell Illustrated, London, 2003.

Matthiessen, Peter, *End of the Earth: Voyages to Antarctica*, National Geographic Society, Washington DC, 2003.

Mawson, Douglas, *Mawson's Antarctic Diaries*, edited by Fred and Eleanor Jacka, Allen & Unwin, Sydney, 1988.

Mill, Hugh Robert, *The Life of Sir Ernest Shackleton*, William Heinemann, London, 1923.

Mills, Leif, *Frank Wild*, Caedmon of Whitby, Whitby, 1999.

Morrell, Margot, and Stephanie Capparell, *Shackleton's Way: leadership lessons from the great Antarctic explorer*, Viking Penguin, New York, 2001.

Murray, George (editor), *The Antarctic Manual: For the use of the expedition of 1901*, Royal Geographical Society, London, 1901.

Murray, James, and George Marston, *Antarctic Days: Sketches of the homely side of Polar life by two of Shackleton's men*, Andrew Melrose, London, 1913.

Paterson, Richard, and Gavin D. Smith, *Goodness Nose: The passionate revelations of a Scotch whisky master blender*, The Angels' Share/Neil Wilson Publishing, Glasgow, 2008.

Peat, Neville, *Antarctic Partners: 50 years of New Zealand and United States cooperation in Antarctica, 1957–2007*, New Zealand Ministry of Foreign Affairs and Trade in association with Phantom House Books, Wellington, 2007.

Peat, Neville, *Looking South: New Zealand Antarctic Society's first fifty years, 1933–83*, New Zealand Antarctic Society, Wellington, 1983.

Peat, Neville, *Snow Dogs: The huskies of Antarctica*, Whitcoulls, Christchurch, 1978.

Priestley, Raymond, *Antarctic Adventure: Scott's Northern Party*, T. Fisher Unwin, London, 1914.

Quartermain, L. B., *New Zealand and the Antarctic*, Government Printer, Wellington, 1971.

Quartermain, L. B., *Two Huts in the Antarctic*, Government Printer, Wellington, 1963.

Ralling, Christopher (introduction), *Shackleton: His Antarctic writings*, British Broadcasting Corporation, London, 1983.

Riffenburgh, Beau, *Nimrod: Ernest Shackleton and the extraordinary story of the 1907–09 British Antarctic Expedition*, Bloomsbury, London, 2004.

Savours, Ann (editor), with an introduction by Sir Peter Scott, *Scott's Last Voyage: Through the Antarctic camera of Herbert Ponting*, Sidgwick and Jackson, London, 1974.

Scott, R. F., *The Voyage of the 'Discovery'*, Volumes I and II, Macmillan and Co., London, 1905.

Shackleton, E. H., *The Heart of the Antarctic: Being the story of the British Antarctic Expedition 1907–1909*, Volumes I and II, William Heinemann, London, 1909.

Shackleton, E. H. (editor), *Aurora Australis*, British Antarctic Expedition 1907–09, Cape Royds, 1908.

Worsley, Henry, *In Shackleton's Footsteps: A return to the heart of the Antarctic*, Virgin Books, London, 2011.

ARTICLES AND REPORTS

Antarctic Heritage Trust, 'Conservation Plan Shackleton's Hut, British Antarctic Expedition 1907–09, Cape Royds, Ross Island', Antarctic Heritage Trust, Christchurch, March 2003.

Blanchette, Robert A., et al., 'An Antarctic hot spot for fungi at Shackleton's historic hut on Cape Royds', *Microbial Ecology* 60, 29–38, April 2010.

Blanchette, Robert A., et al., 'Environmental pollutants from the Scott and Shackleton expeditions during the "heroic age" of Antarctic exploration', *Polar Record* 40(2), 143–151, 2004.

Blanchette, Robert A., et al., 'Wood-destroying soft rot fungi in the historic expedition huts of Antarctica', *Applied and Environmental Microbiology* 70(3), 1328–1335, 2004.

Blanchette, Robert A., Benjamin W. Held, and Roberta L. Farrell, 'Defibration of wood in the expedition huts of Antarctica: an unusual deterioration process occurring in the polar environment', *Polar Record* 38(207), 313–322, 2002.

Farrell, Roberta L., et al., 'Scientific evaluation of deterioration of historic huts of Ross Island, Antarctica', in S. Barr and B. Chaplin (editors), *Historical Polar Bases: Preservation and management*, ICOMOS Monuments and Sites No. XVII, International Polar Heritage Committee, Oslo, Norway, 2008.

Priestley, Rebecca, 'Ernest Shackleton's 100-year-old Whisky', *New Zealand Listener*, 29 October 2011.

Pryde, James, et al., 'Sensory and chemical analysis of 'Shackleton's' Mackinlay Scotch whisky', *Journal of the Institute of Brewing* 117(2), 156–165, 2011.

WEBSITES AND LINKS

Whisky sites

www.whyteandmackay.co.uk (home page of Whyte & Mackay whisky)

http://www.youtube.com/watch?v=j4xK1HsFWOY&feature=player_embedded#at=49 (video story of Mackinlay's, the Nimrod expedition and the return of the bottles of whisky to Scotland)

http://www.youtube.com/watch?v=uYerEDUzNag&NR=1 (TVOne news clip about the rediscovery of the whisky)

www.scotch-whisky.org.uk (home page of the Scotch Whisky Association)

www.scotchwhisky.net (source offering 'the most comprehensive, accurate and "up to date" information regarding Scotch whisky and the Scotch whisky industry')

www.whiskydistilled.com (online enthusiasts' guide to whisky/whiskey)

Antarctic sites

www.heritage-antarctica.org (home page of the New Zealand Antarctic
  Heritage Trust)

www.antarcticanz.govt.nz (home page of Antarctica New Zealand)

www.jamescairdsociety.com (home page of the James Caird Society, a
  charitable institution dedicated to the memory of Shackleton and
  Antarctic exploration)

www.antarctic-circle.org (home page of the Antarctic Circle, an
  historical–cultural forum and resource on all things Antarctican)

Acknowledgements

The people I need to thank for information, photographs and support, and there are scores of them, fall largely into two groups — Antarctic contacts and those who belong to the world of whisky.

Before I could embark on a solid year's work to complete this project I needed financial encouragement. It arrived from an unexpected source, an American couple seeking to photograph all of the world's 19 penguin species: Clinton and Missy Kelly, of Bethesda, Maryland. Both are admirers of Ernest Shackleton and both have visited Antarctica. I met them on a subantarctic expedition when they were pursuing their last species, the erect-crested penguin of Antipodes Island. Their contribution to the cost of research and, in particular, the fieldwork in England and Scotland kick-started the project. Heartfelt thanks.

My main Antarctic contacts were at the Antarctic Heritage Trust in Christchurch — Executive Director Nigel Watson, Programme Manager and Conservation Team Leader Al Fastier, Programme Manager Artefacts Lizzie Meek, and Communications and Events Manager Paula Granger. I am grateful for their unstinting support, information, photographs and proofreading. I also thank Antarctica New Zealand's chief executive Lou Sanson for permission to reproduce several maps and photographs. Antarctic historians David Harrowfield (Oamaru), Baden Norris (Christchurch) and Robert Headland (Cambridge) gave me research leads and inspiration. Harold Lowe, of Gore, an Antarctic enthusiast and a New Zealand Antarctic Research Programme colleague of mine from 1975–76, kindly lent me his precious copy of *The Heart of the Antarctic* (1909, first edition, two volumes), signed by Sir James Mills, chairman and managing director of the Union Steam Ship Company. For details of their Cape Royds exploits in the early years of the New Zealand Antarctic Research Programme, I am indebted to biologists Rowley Taylor, Euan Young and Oliver Sutherland, all of Nelson.

In London, Hon. Alexandra Shackleton, president of the James Caird Society, welcomed my enquiries about her grandfather, as did Johnny Van Haeften, the grand-nephew of Sir Philip Brocklehurst. In Sydney, on my behalf, Alister Robinson delved deeply into the archives of the Mitchell Library/State Library of New South Wales, to unearth information on 1907–09 British Antarctic Expedition participants Professor T. W. Edgeworth David and Douglas Mawson.

For advice on preserving timber structures in Antarctica I turned to two specialists, Professor Robert A. Blanchette (University of Minnesota) and Professor Roberta Farrell (University of Waikato) and thank them for checking my interpretations. Canterbury Museum staff Sasha Stollman, Natalie Cadenhead and Kelvin Nolly briefed me on the technical challenges of the museum's 'Great Whisky Crate Thaw' project. At the University of Otago in Dunedin I received advice from Associate Professor Pat Langhorne (Physics Department) about sea ice, and Associate Professor David Gerrard (School of Medicine) about the effects of alcohol on people exposed to extreme cold. Don Whyte (Dunedin) briefed me on New Zealand postage stamps of the Edwardian era. Paul Sagar lent a copy of the Fisher biography of Ernest Shackleton, and Delyth Sunley, Clare Greensmith and Ian Farquhar provided useful information. In the United Kingdom, Scott Polar Research Institute Archives Manager Naomi Boneham introduced me to a series of unpublished diaries, and Adelie penguin scientist David Ainley (California) updated me on the southernmost penguin colonies.

For general guidance on the world of whisky I thank Michael Fraser-Milne, owner of Whisky Galore, Christchurch, and staff members Dave Armstrong and Stephen Le Petit. From Whyte & Mackay, of Glasgow, came consistent support. Master blender Richard Paterson treated me to a short course on whisky tasting, Chief Chemist Dr James Pryde explained the intricacies of chemical analysis, and Global PR Director Rob Bruce offered strategic advice. Veteran whisky writer Dave Broom, the only independent taster of both the original whisky and the replica, provided an independent critique of the replica, as did a small group of Mackinlay descendants — Donald, Ian and Nial Mackinlay. It was a privilege to meet the three of them in their home valley near Pitlochry. Their New Zealand-based cousin, Charles Mackinlay Usher (Kaiapoi, North Canterbury), added details of the family heritage in whisky. Peter Lankester (Bratton, Wiltshire) educated me about the Royal Navy rum tradition and put the Shackleton whisky into context, and Jazz Hamilton of Scotia Bar and Café in Dunedin and Dunedin whisky taster David Barnes provided useful information.

The illustrations in the book were acquired from more than 25 sources. The Antarctic Heritage Trust (Al Fastier, Lizzie Meek, Paula Granger, Nigel McCall and others) contributed images of the hut conservation work and whisky recovery. Canterbury Museum (Dr Kerry McCarthy, Nic Boigelot), Scott Polar Research

Institute (Lucy Martin) and the Royal Geographical Society (Joy Wheeler) provided a swag of images from the Nimrod expedition. I also thank Whyte & Mackay for the photographs of the original whisky on its return to Scotland. Thanks also to Rowley Taylor, Euan Young and Oliver Sutherland, as well as surveyor Frank Graveson, for the images from their time at Cape Royds. Other contributors were Antarctica New Zealand, James Blake, Robert A. Blanchette, Dunedin Public Library (Anthony Tedeschi), David Harrowfield, the Mackinlay family, Scott Jennings, Mitchell Library/State Library of New South Wales, Mark Orams, Julian Paren, Phil Reimer/United States Navy, Charles Usher, Eric Wedgewood, Adam Wild and Lieutenant-Colonel Henry Worsley. Allan Kynaston drew the map of the Southern Journey and Scott's Farthest South.

My thanks also to the British High Commissioner in New Zealand, Vicki Treadell, who is part of the story, and to Helen Fawthorpe in the Ministry of Foreign Affairs and Trade's Antarctic Policy Unit. For splendid hospitality in England and Scotland, I am indebted to David Garcia and Sue Jones, Roger and Gill Smaridge, Chris and Sue Weeks, Mary Loukes, Jean and Sandy Lindsay, Ian and Isobel Mackinlay, and Margaret Somerville and Mike Kendall.

My wife, Mary Hammonds, was a stalwart research assistant, helping me navigate around England and Scotland. On the publishing front, I thank commissioning editor Barbara Larson, project manager Kate Stone and the Random House production team, and editor Matt Turner, who did an expert job of polishing and straightening up the text.

Index